Managing Finance, Premises and Health & Safety

Also available:

Steps in Leadership
Huw Thomas
978-1-84312-434-4
1-84312-434-3

Inspection and Accountability
Bill Laar
978-1-84312-436-8
1-84312-436-X

Inclusion
Linda Evans
978-1-84312-453-5
1-84312-453-X

Making the Most of Your Headship
Gerald Haigh and Anne Perry
978-1-84312-435-1
1-84312-435-1

Managing Finance, Premises and Health & Safety

David Miller, John Plant and Paul Scaife

Routledge
Taylor & Francis Group

LONDON AND NEW YORK

First published 2007
by Routledge
2 Park Square, Milton Park, Abingdon, Oxon, OX14 4RN

Simultaneously published in the USA and Canada by Routledge
711 Third Ave, New York, NY 10017

Routledge is an imprint of the Taylor & Francis Group, an informa business

© 2007 David Miller, John Plant and Paul Scaife

Note: The right of David Miller, John Plant and Paul Scaife to be
identified as the authors of this work has been asserted by them in
accordance with the Copyright, Designs and Patents Act 1988.

Typeset by RefineCatch Limited, Bungay, Suffolk

British Library Cataloguing in Publication Data
A catalogue record for this book is available from the British Library

Library of Congress Cataloging in Publication Data
A catalog record for this book has been requested

ISBN10: 1-84312-454-8
ISBN13: 978-1-84312-454-2

Contents

Foreword

Headteachers and governors of local authority schools have been managing their own school budgets for a quarter of a century or so now. It's difficult to imagine a time when nearly all the money was centrally controlled, and just about the only choices open to heads were around what sort of pencils, books and chalk to order.

Now, although budgets are often tight, at least schools are free to use them not just efficiently – that's a basic essential – but with enough imagination and foresight to ensure the best possible outcomes for their children.

Some heads, of course, find it difficult to come to terms with the management tasks around money, buildings, health and safety and furniture. They have trouble accepting that a career spent developing as a teacher culminates, at the top, in a multi-faceted management post that involves not just organising the curriculum but financing it. On top of that there's a building to worry about, and the health and safety of everyone who uses it. 'I didn't become a teacher to do all this!' is the cry.

As this book makes crystal clear, however, that isn't the point at all. The child sitting at a desk embarking on the day's work is at the focus of a range of resourcing decisions. Is it a good desk? Or is it wobbly, irritating, potentially dangerous and about to fall to bits because someone missed the opportunity to buy when prices were low? Is there an electronic whiteboard in the room, or was the money spent on a new minibus that might have been better leased? Is the class being taught French by a non-specialist because of a misjudged staffing decision two years before? Is everyone freezing because the energy policy's gone off the rails?

Schools will inevitably make wrong-footed moves from time to time – they're organic institutions, dealing with fickle human beings. But effective leadership and management will keep the faulty thinking to a minimum. The aim is to ensure that the child is at the best possible desk in a well-equipped, well-heated room, being taught in safe comfort by the best possible teacher. And it's no good saying that the decisions leading up to this happy state aren't educational, because they quite obviously are. Just ask the child and the teacher if you're not sure.

To our authors, David Miller, John Plant and Paul Scaife, the logic is crystal clear. So although their book is a highly practical guide through the complications of finance and resources, there's never any doubt about the core purpose.

'Throughout this,' they write, 'we have never forgotten that the focus of schools is teaching and learning and have ensured that clear links are made between school goals and resource management.'

No head, presumably, would disagree with that. It's just that under pressure it's possible to stray away from the procedures that make it happen. In how many schools, for example, does annual budgeting consist of looking at last year's budget headings and then trimming a bit here and adding something there? Even though everyone in the school knows that the starting point should be the school development plan? It's not done from indolence or neglect, of course. It's about pressure, time and above all, perhaps, the lack of a no-nonsense adviser giving some prods and some words of advice.

Well, here are three no-nonsense advisers, ready to help you. Work with them, and next year you might come out of the budgeting process without the nagging feeling that maybe you could be doing a bit better.

Gerald Haigh 2007

Acknowledgements

The authors would like to thank: Adrian Pierce and Janet Tomlinson for their help with the manuscript; Anoop Rughani, Andrew Bownes and Martin Wood for their advice on premises issues; and Claire Hallam and Alan Rowe for their advice on health and safety issues.

Introduction

Money is a needful and precious thing, and when well used, a noble thing, but I never want you to think it is the first or only prize to strive for.

(Louisa M. Alcott, *Little Women*)

We have worked closely for many years with headteachers, and in our experience when they gather together and financial and premises matters are raised, three familiar themes emerge.

First, some heads still believe that funding is inadequate, and many would concur that the funding regime is complicated. The BBC once memorably described it as 'fiendishly complex'. The Department for Education and Skills (DfES) has been working towards making funding simpler and there are positive signs that this will continue in the next few years. For example, the School Standards Grant and Standards Fund are being merged.

DfES ministers and officials would also point to above inflation rises in per pupil funding over the last ten years, plus considerable resources for capital improvements to buildings. Some heads would probably respond by saying that the positive effects of the extra funding have been uneven across the country, and that falling rolls, rising employee and utility costs and the loss of key grants have watered them down.

Second, many heads would be concerned that managing finances and the building can be a time-consuming distraction from the key task of leading the teaching and learning of the school. They would rightly suggest that they should only be tools to enable the successful delivery of managing achievement. They would surely agree with Louisa M. Alcott that money should not be the only prize to strive for. Despite this, all too often budgetary management can appear to be the driver of the goals of the school, rather than the other way round.

Finally, the bureaucracy heads face would probably concern them. They would point to almost daily updates of legislation, guidance and rules, many of them designed to manage risks and to counter the 'compensation culture' we all live in.

This book is intended to be a practical guide to the management of school resources. We have attempted to provide you with useful tools, tips and ideas that can be used

- to assess your current resource management;
- to make realistic plans for the future; and
- to monitor, control and review your resources over the financial year.

Throughout this, we have never forgotten that the focus of schools is teaching and learning and have ensured that clear links are made between school goals and resource management.

There is only a limited amount we can do to help you enhance your general funding, so we have focused on helping you make the best use of your resources. We have tried to be sparing in our references to legislation and rules, only quoting them when they are crucial to understanding the issues. We refer to sources of information, particularly on the Internet, so that you can undertake further research if you need to.

The sheer volume of material on health and safety has meant that we have only been able to refer to the key issues. You may want to delve further into the legislation and guidance for more on this topic.

We have focused closely on the DfES Financial Management Standard and Toolkit as it seems likely that primary schools will face some kind of assessment, probably external, against the Standard over the next few years. As we write, the exact assessment process is subject to DfES consultation with primary schools. We have therefore used the

Standard as a theme throughout the book to enable you to make connections to it and begin to plan your actions.

One issue highlighted in the Standard, and a common feature in schools having resource problems, is the inadequacy of their long-term planning. We encourage you to plan your resource management using the techniques we recommend in the book. Although resource planning is an inexact science, it can help schools avoid the most severe effects of shortage of resources.

We do not recommend that you follow the advice of our favourite financial expert, Charles Dickens' Mr Micawber, who hoped that 'something will turn up'.

David Miller
John Plant
Paul Scaife

October 2006

Chapter 1
Taking stock

Annual income twenty pounds, annual expenditure nineteen pounds nineteen shillings and sixpence, result happiness. Annual income twenty pounds, annual expenditure twenty pounds and sixpence, result misery.

(Mr Micawber in Charles Dickens' *David Copperfield*)

Misery!

Many headteachers will be familiar with Mr Micawber's theory of resource management, particularly those who have limited funds. Some may choose to follow his philosophy of escaping from their problems by waiting for something to turn up. Fortunately they are likely to avoid debtor's prison, unlike their role model, but the resulting misery of redundancies, shortage of equipment and materials, and consequent local publicity can be nearly as painful.

This book sets out a systematic approach to avoiding such misery by giving you practical tips for improving your management of resources. However, in doing this, we need to take a rather more sophisticated approach to our definition of resource management than Mr Micawber takes. It is not enough that you spend within your budget; you need to consider how you spend your budget. We will challenge you to evaluate whether the objectives of the school are properly reflected in your expenditure.

Many shrewd governors will ask their headteachers to explain how the budget they have set will achieve the objectives set out in the School Development Plan (SDP). This is a proper question for them to ask – to make sure they fulfil their role as a critical friend and are accountable for the school budget. Unfortunately, some heads struggle to answer the question, and the way that accounts are publicly presented is not straightforward, and therefore not much help to the head.

When the school budget is analysed, some schools are unable to demonstrate that they are earmarking resources to meet their objectives. Indeed, because some schools plan their budgets using a historical model, they find that resources are being utilised for purposes entirely different than the current objectives. A school may declare that their major priority is to improve the literacy of the pupils when the hard reality is that money is being spent on design and technology.

The financial management cycle

To help take a more strategic approach to the use of resources, we will follow a model that has been around for many years but is still valid (Figure 1.1).

Essentially, good resource management means deploying your resources carefully to ensure you can meet the objectives in the

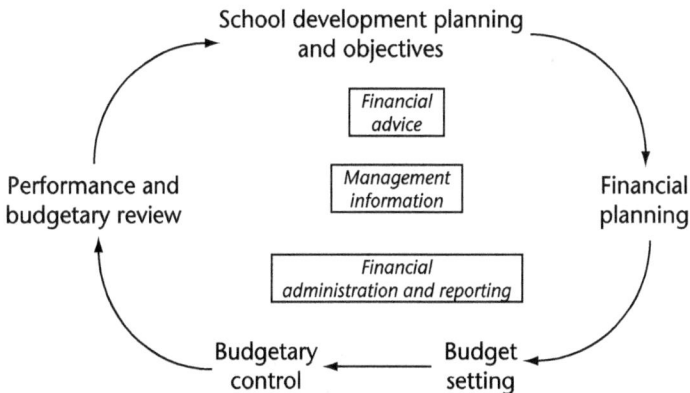

Figure 1.1   The financial management cycle

SDP, achieve best value and undertake activities that the school can afford.

The estimated cost of achieving the SDP objectives and planned cost of maintaining the school's existing provision should be shown in a financial plan. This plan should ideally cover a three-year period at least. You should build anticipated income for the three-year period into the plan and compare these with estimated costs, to determine if the school's plans are affordable. If the plans are not affordable, you will need to:

- review the SDP objectives;

- consider alternative, more cost-effective ways of achieving the SDP objectives;

- pursue additional sources of income.

Keep in mind that long-term financial planning is an inexact science. Even with the DfES Dedicated Schools Grant (DSG), it is likely that future funding will inevitably be somewhat different from that originally anticipated.

The school's annual budget should reflect the first year of your long-term plan. The budget sets the annual income and expenditure targets that a school needs to meet if it is going to deliver planned provision in an affordable way. Actual income and expenditure should be monitored against the budget regularly, with any big differences being controlled and reviewed as the financial year progresses. The success of this process depends on:

- the effectiveness of the school's financial administration and accounting systems;

- a strong culture of financial responsibility and accountability at all levels in the school; and

- effective leadership, challenge and support to the financial management process by the governing body and leadership team.

The DfES Financial Management Standard and Toolkit (FMSiS)

Our route map for this journey will be the FMSiS. Published in 2004 and updated in 2005 and 2006, FMSiS sets the standard for financial management in schools and provides a wealth of relevant guidance for schools on how to manage their resources. It includes a toolkit to help schools reach the standard and improve.

FMSiS also includes a comprehensive self-assessment tool to enable you to evaluate your own management of resources. Although this can be a time-consuming process, it is straightforward to break FMSiS down into constituent parts and evaluate your resource management systematically. The five main parts of FMSiS are:

- leadership and governance;
- people management;
- policy and strategy;
- partnerships and resources;
- processes.

We shall refer to relevant parts of FMSiS throughout this book.

Some of the headings may appear to have little to do with the subject in hand, but FMSiS consciously takes a broader approach, one that Mr Micawber sadly missed. At present, use of FMSiS is still discretionary for primaries, but the DfES is likely to make both self- and external assessment mandatory for such schools in the next few years. FMSiS is available on www.fmsis.info.

Stocktaking and PESTE analysis

A useful way to begin to review the use of resources in a school is to think about the school environment, which can lead to review of the effectiveness of the SDP. A PESTE (political, economic, social,

Table 1.1 One school's PESTE analysis

Political	Economic	Social	Technological	Environmental
Government White Paper on education	Dedicated schools budget	Demolition of local housing estate	Broadband internet	Recycling initiative in local authority
Local political priorities on key stage 2	Rising energy costs	Influx of asylum seekers to area	Electronic connection to local authorities	New road system could present safety hazards to pupils
Workforce reform	Pay awards	Vandalism	New payroll system	Litter on playing field

technological and environmental) analysis is excellent for this and focuses attention on the factors facing the school. There are several different versions of PESTE.

In the example in Table 1.1, the headteacher analysed the factors facing the school and divided them into the five PESTE categories (some factors may run into more than one category). The next step would be to think about when and how these factors are likely to affect the school and what the resulting costs might be, and use this information as a basis for assumptions in the financial plan.

Reviewing the previous year

The summer term is the ideal time for schools to begin to review their use of the previous financial year's resources. Look at those areas where there was a significant difference between what you planned to spend and what you actually spent. Try to understand the reasons why this happened; will it happen again in the current year or was it a 'one-off'? This review should throw up any 'pinch points' – places where budget heads did not have sufficient resources allocated at the start of the financial year or there were control issues. The review should also help identify areas of recurring costs you had not planned for in the past but will need to plan for in the future. For example:

- Did you cut down on supply because of a new cover assistant but have a spate of days when two or even three colleagues were absent?

- Did you find that repair bills were much lower than previous years because the new security system cut the cost of vandalism?

The review needs to be more than just an examination of whether more or less money has been spent than expected. It can also help show if the school's development and planning objectives have been achieved (see Figure 1.1).

> Tip – Never just look at the money! Your review should include what the money was spent on and how well it matched up to the needs of the school.

Be very specific when you evaluate expenditure against objectives, for example:

- Has the expenditure spent on the building had the desired effect? Is the roof watertight?

- Does the boiler work satisfactorily now? Has that ground maintenance contractor given good value for money?

- Has the extra money you ploughed into literacy had the desired effect?

- £6,000 was spent on the library – does your self-evaluation shown that children are reading for pleasure?

- Was there a reason for a particular level of sickness absence among a group of staff?

- Did you save money by changing your Sickness Absence Insurance provider? Would alternative arrangements have been more cost-effective?

The results of your review should inform your planning discussions for the following year. You can use the information you gathered in this process in your school's self-evaluation form (SEF) for Ofsted.

However, that isn't the end of the review. You also need to take in to consideration the balances you hold as a school. Remember that you have been given your delegated budget to use for the education of the children you have now, not to save for some unspecific rainy day in the future. In 2004, the Audit Commission pointed out that there were national surpluses of over £1 billion in English schools. Since then authorities have become more stringent about asking schools to justify holding large surplus balances.

Where you have a deficit balance it is crucial that clear plans are established for bringing your school back to a balanced position. A useful exercise that you can do in the autumn term is benchmark your previous year's spending against similar schools. There is a national schools benchmarking website available to schools on the Teachernet website (www.teachernet.gov.uk/schoolfinance). On the site, you can select schools of an equivalent size in other areas and compare how much you have spent on different budget headings, in both percentage of the budget and cost per pupil terms. (Details of how to use the site are in Chapter 2.) Of course, this information may raise more questions than answers. You may find that you spend 2 per cent more than the national average on teachers and £3 per pupil less on premises. You may have a perfectly good reason for this, but learning this fact may throw up issues that you had not considered, and these can then be usefully discussed with the governing body.

In addition, some local authorities also publish benchmarking information, often on their website, that enables schools to compare their costs against those of similar schools. The advantage of this information at the local level is that you can select schools you know rather than anonymous national schools. If you have questions about use of resources, you can contact the head to seek further background information or even arrange a visit. Further information about benchmarking is in section 3.2 of FMSiS.

Reviewing your current budget

We have mentioned the importance of monitoring actual spending against the budget to get a picture of how your budget is doing. You may want to focus on the crucial issue of reviewing the teaching and learning in the school, but you shouldn't rely too heavily on your administrative officers to keep finance on track.

Some heads do struggle to understand budget-monitoring sheets, and you might believe that you will have to put up with what is provided. However, many current accounting packages allow you to drop figures into a spreadsheet, remove surplus information and provide a commentary in words. In Chapters 4 and 5 we will look at this in more detail and discuss alternative spreadsheet models.

An excellent document to assist you in your stocktaking of how the budget is being spent, is the income and expenditure checklist for primary schools, prepared by the National Remodelling Team and available through the National College for School Leadership (NCSL) website (www.ncsl.org.uk). Not only will this checklist give you further ideas on benchmarking, it provides a whole series of invaluable questions to ask yourself about the use of expenditure and even generation of income. This resource is worth sharing with the leadership team of the school.

Assessment of the school's building issues

In 2000, the DfES asked local authorities to collect data on the condition of their schools. Many of the local authorities took this as an opportunity to produce asset management plans for schools to help them identify the major priorities for the school building. Some local authorities will still assess the school and draw up a plan as part of their support service. If this service is not available to you, ask a private surveyor or experienced building superintendent – they should be able to produce something similar.

This assessment and plan should identify:

- the condition and suitability of the building for achieving the objectives of the school;

- the main priorities for the short- and long-term maintenance of the building health and safety issues.

It should also set out a timeline for addressing the issues identified and a schedule of costs likely to be incurred. Figures 1.2 and 1.3 are fictional examples from Holly Lane primary school.

Some heads might argue that the cost of such an assessment is an unacceptable additional one, but it can assist greatly with the management of risk. In the compensation culture we all live in today, it is vital to be clear about what risks the school building carries. More importantly, it gives you an opportunity to plan your premises investments over the next few years and consider how you might utilise your capital formula grant and your building maintenance and improvement revenue funds. We will cover this in more detail in Chapter 2.

> All the toilets and some of the corridor areas have been rewired with new distribution boards and fittings in the last year. The rest of it is over 30 years old and will need replacing within 2 years. The ICT area is in a corridor and is a temporary installation. The lighting is fluorescent it will require renewing along with the wiring. The fire alarm is a stand-alone manual system but due to its age and non-compliance with British Standards should be replaced with a system complying with BS5839. The emergency lighting is a central battery system but due to its age and condition it has not been connected to the newer fittings, which are stand-alone bulkheads. The system should be replaced with one complying with BS5226. The security system is a PIR stand-alone and CCTV covers the main entrance with a monitor in the reception and headmistress's office. The rest of the doors are locked.

Figure 1.2 Assessment of the Old Oak Building, Holly Lane primary school

The chart below displays the total forecast expenditure need for the whole property based on the condition survey. Each cost is summarised against the standard element description as defined by the DfES. The costs are subtotalled by priority one, two and three to indicate the urgency of the work required (where one is the most urgent).

Element	Priority one	Priority two	Priority three	Total
1 Roofs	£5,369	£24,126	£1,652	**£31,147**
2 Floors		£4,499	£724	**£5,223**
3 Ceilings		£126		**£126**
4 External walls	£225	£11,054	£3,155	**£14,434**
5 Internal floors and doors	£504	£561	£10,541	**£11,606**
6 Mechanical services		£418	£233,610	**£234,028**
7 Electrical services			£244,045	**£244,045**
8 Redecorations		£1,464	£7,276	**£8,740**
9 External areas	£126	£261	£8,039	**£8,426**
Grand total	**£6,224**	**£42,509**	**£509,042**	**£557,775**

Figure 1.3   Holly Lane Primary: cost summary by element

Assessing health and safety risks

Responsibility for health and safety depends on who is the employer. For community schools it rests with the local authority; for foundation and voluntary aided schools with the governing body. In the former, the local authority will inevitably have a legitimate interest in the health and safety of both staff and students. However, this does not mean that heads or governors can absolve themselves of responsibility. In the event of a serious accident it is likely that your policies and actions will be closely scrutinised, possibly even in court.

Headteachers have been prosecuted recently, sometimes with the local authority and a building contractor. Case law suggests that even when a headteacher is unaware of a safety hazard he or she cannot abdicate responsibility. For example, a contractor entering a school should sign the asbestos register to show that they are aware of any risk in this area. The register needs to be up to date and action taken to make contractors aware of the risk. If the contractor were to uncover asbestos and leave it exposed, the head could be as culpable as the contractor.

Staff also carry responsibility for health and safety under the health and safety legislation of 1974 and 1999, both for themselves and others. It is not unknown for inspectors from the Health and Safety Executive to turn up unannounced at a school and conduct inspections. Serious breaches of the regulations have occasionally also led to prosecutions of local authorities, schools and individuals, particularly where electricity or gas were concerned.

Virtually all heads will however be less worried about the enactment of the regulatory framework or potential for financial claims than the actual injury to staff or pupils. Whether this is a minor burn to a teacher in the staff room, or broken bones from the caretaker falling from a high ladder inadequately secured, it is a subject that should take high priority in your agenda.

There are four steps you should take to achieve excellence in health and safety:

■ Create a positive health and safety culture – staff need to take ownership of the subject and be fully aware of their role in promoting safety. Including health and safety in the induction of new employees, and providing regular systematic training can achieve this. You also need to update staff about changes in legislation or new hazards.

■ Promote a healthy and safe working environment, both for staff and students – arrange for regular health and safety audits, ideally by you, but possibly by other leadership team members with a clear responsibility, and inspecting buildings regularly. These should be done at least once a year, more frequently in special circumstances, such as during a large building project, or if the building undergoes significant change of use. Community schools need to arrange for the local authority or alternative qualified health and safety officer to monitor their work. Foundation schools will probably wish to seek advice and guidance.

■ Take a proactive approach to managing risk. The days when parents were happy to accept that their beloved offspring simply fell and hurt themselves are long gone. You need a robust risk-assessment procedure.

■ Comply fully with the relevant regulatory framework. Make sure that you regularly consult appropriate health and safety professionals for advice and assistance.

There is a particularly useful section on health and safety, covering policy, inspection, safe practice, and security on Teachernet (www.teachernet.gov.uk).

▪ Terminology

One of the obstacles you may encounter when you are trying to understand the school's use of resources is jargon. Simple concepts can be made impenetrable by the use of mystifying terms. What are 'variances', 'profiling', and 'liability'? How can figures be negative? What is CFR?

You may even be unclear about the difference between revenue and capital funds. Table 1.2 contains a jargonbuster to help you understand some of the most common financial terms you will encounter.

Table 1.2 Jargonbuster of financial terms

Financial term	Definition
Asset	A valuable item that is owned by the school *or* an amount owed to a school, normally at the end of a financial year, such as money to be paid from an insurance claim.
Audit trail	Evidence linking successive steps in a process, such as the purchase of supplies.
Capital expenditure	Spending which produces an asset, usually with a long life and/or high value, such as a new building or a minibus.
Capital Formula Grant	A devolved grant, made available through the local authority and earmarked for capital building projects.
Carryforward	Amount overspent or underspent against a school's budget, which must in law be carried forward and added to or deducted from the following year's income.
Commitment	Expenditure to which the school is committed but not yet paid, such as outstanding orders.
Consistent Financial Reporting Framework (CFR)	A way of consistently recording schools' income and expenditure across the country to facilitate benchmarking.
Delegated budget	Funds allocated by the local authority, driven by formula, which become the responsibility of the schools.
Earmarked budget	Money allocated to a school for a defined purpose, liable to be returned to the local authority if unspent on that purpose, such as a capital formula grant for large building projects.
Fixed costs	Costs that will be incurred regardless of the level of production or service provided, such as business rates.

Forecast outturn	Your estimate of where you are going to be at the end of the financial year, which will include projections of income and expenditure.
Liability	Amount owed by the school, normally at the end of a financial year, such as an invoice that has not been paid.
Profiling	A process by which a budget is divided up over the financial year to give an accurate reflection of spending or income patterns, such as the cost of energy.
Revenue expenditure	Spending of a day-to-day nature, such as teachers' salaries or cleaning materials.
Tender	Procedure for inviting potential suppliers to offer their services competitively, usually used above a certain price level, such as £25k or £50k.
Variable costs	Costs that vary according to the level of production or service provided, such as gas.
Variance	The difference between actual expenditure (or income) and budgeted expenditure (or income) at a given point in time.

Chapter 2
Planning ahead

*'Would you tell me, please, which way I ought to go from here?'
asked Alice. 'That depends a good deal on where you want to
get to,' said the cat. 'I don't care where . . .' said Alice. 'Then it
doesn't matter which way you go,' said the cat.*

(Lewis Carroll, *Alice in Wonderland*)

Why do a financial plan?

DfES expectations are that schools should take a more strategic
approach to their budgets in line with the introduction of the three-year
funding in the form of the DSG from April 2006 (see section 3.9 of
FMSiS). There is a clear expectation that schools will plan their funding
levels and resourcing requirements over three years and that this
planning will be linked the to the SDP. It also makes clear that the
SDP should be 'consistent with any longer term financial plans for
recovering deficits or saving up for future developments' (section 3.1 of
FMSiS).

However, there are good *practical* reasons for producing a multi-year
financial plan. Multi-year planning helps a school model longer-term
aims and objectives and identify financial implications and financial
risks. Many schools stumble into deficit and have to take short-term
drastic action, when such problems could have been anticipated and
dealt with incrementally. In particular, multi-year planning can give an
early indication of the future impact of reductions in pupil numbers, a

problem in many primary schools across the country. Since one of the key governance roles is 'strategic direction', it is crucial that governors have a clear idea of these resourcing requirements.

Multi-year financial planning provides an opportunity to take a more strategic approach to decision-making based on longer-term financial projections. For example, a teacher resignation may lead to replacements, but if rolls are falling this may be a temporary measure.

All too often, the annual budget-setting process is a rushed (and sometimes painful) process. Moving to an autumn-term planning process spreads the financial workload more evenly across the year. A long-term financial planning approach should make the annual budget process a simple 'tidying up and review' exercise, once the precise funding figures based on the Pupil Level Annual Schools Census (PLASC) return are known.

Five steps to producing a financial plan

We will use a five-step model for producing a financial plan (Figure 2.1).

Step 1: Gathering the strategic information

It is best not to dive straight into preparing a financial plan until you have a clear understanding of the longer-term strategic plans for the school and have worked out the likely cost of achieving these plans. Information can be gathered from many sources including discussions with governors. Ideally, you should be able to make use of the following plans that are commonly found in schools to gather information about what the school is planning to do:

- School Development Plan (SDP).

- Classroom Organisation Plan.

- Workforce Reform Plan.

- Risk Management Plan.

- Asset Management Plan.

- Extended School Activity Plan.

```
┌─────────────────────────────────────────┐
│ STEP 1                                    │
│                                           │
│ Gathering the strategic information       │
└─────────────────────────────────────────┘
                    │
                    ▼
┌─────────────────────────────────────────┐
│ STEP 2                                    │
│                                           │
│ Agreeing the planning assumptions         │
└─────────────────────────────────────────┘
                    │
                    ▼
┌─────────────────────────────────────────┐
│ STEP 3                                    │
│                                           │
│ Understanding your financial position     │
└─────────────────────────────────────────┘
                    │
                    ▼
┌─────────────────────────────────────────┐
│ STEP 4                                    │
│                                           │
│         Building a financial plan         │
└─────────────────────────────────────────┘
                    │
                    ▼
┌─────────────────────────────────────────┐
│ STEP 5                                    │
│                                           │
│         Using the financial plan          │
└─────────────────────────────────────────┘
```

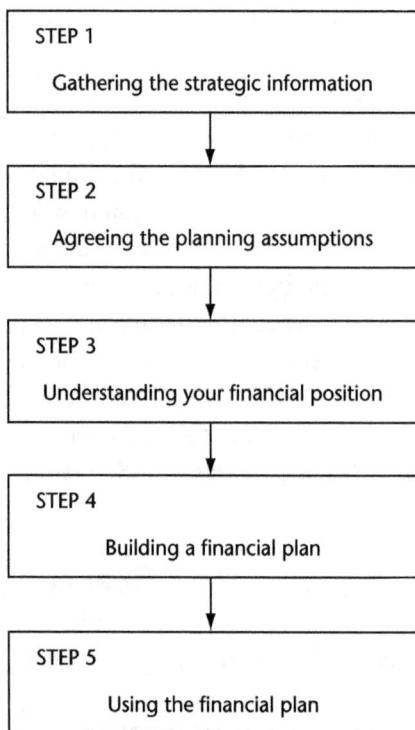

Figure 2.1   A five-step model for producing a financial plan

If you do not have access to actual plans, you need to assemble the kind of information that would be included in such plans. Having gathered information on the school's plans for the future you will need to work out when the planned actions would happen and how much they would cost.

Costing the SDP
The objectives of the school should be properly described in the SDP. Costing these objectives is often only partially done. Where educational equipment and learning resources are needed for an objective, these can be straightforward to cost. Costs can be divided into four basic types:

■   labour;

■   equipment;

■ expenses;

■ overheads.

Table 2.1 shows an example of a costing exercise – a school that is proposing to introduce foreign languages into its curriculum.

All costs – direct and indirect – should be included. For example, support staff time is often seen as an inexhaustible commodity, treated as an indirect cost and not included in costs. If salary costs are to be included, related costs such as National Insurance and superannuation should also be included. Other costs related to personnel, such as phone calls, mileage claims and equipment can be easily overlooked. Support costs, for example, for photocopying and printing, are frequently omitted. All these costs, if not included, can appear as overspends later in the year and be hard to justify.

Table 2.1   Cost of introducing foreign languages into the school curriculum

Foreign languages	Estimated cost
Direct labour costs	
Preparation of curriculum materials by co-ordinator	£250
Training of teachers	£250
Equipment	
CDs	£50
Books	£100
Expenses	
Photocopying of activity sheets	£50
Small adaptation to classroom 3	£200
Overheads	
Electricity	£50
Support staff costs – photocopying of activity sheets	£100
Total	**£1,050**

Other strategic information

Where schools have access to an Asset Management Plan, this should also be costed, as described in Chapter 1. The staffing structure devised under the Workforce Reforms should also be to hand, with any planned changes. Salary costs should be calculated in detail. A comprehensive attempt to produce a multi-year financial plan will help challenge the appropriateness and affordability of your staffing structure for the next few years.

Classroom Organisation Plans are not common in primary schools, but it is worth analysing how you deploy teaching and learning staff in delivering the curriculum, particularly if your pupil numbers are falling and funding looks fragile. Many schools also need to think about the funding and costs that are related to the Extended Schools initiative. Ideally a business plan should be devised to deliver this. The DfES has produced useful information on this, which can be downloaded from Teachernet.

Step 2: Agreeing the planning assumptions

After gathering the strategic information, it is essential to agree and clearly document assumptions about variable financial and non-financial factors that may affect financial plans. These assumptions are an integral part of constructing a financial plan and will affect the financial outcomes shown on the plan. Many schools will produce several financial plans based on different assumptions before making any key strategic decision. For example you may want to look at the impact of different assumptions about pupil numbers on the school's income before making a decision about the school's longer-term staffing structure.

Basic planning assumptions should include:

■ Pay and price inflation – This information should be available through your local authority. It does however raise the issue of whether it is necessary to use inflation at all. The worst thing you can do is to inflate your income figures for the next few years, probably using projected government data, but not to inflate your expenditure in a similar way. This can lead to a dangerous false sense of security. You might consider leaving everything at today's price levels and look at the volume changes affecting the school, for example, changes in pupil numbers. However, if you do decide to inflate figures in future years, check with your local authority about what inflation assumptions they are using. The local authority financial support service should be able to give you guidance.

■ Pupil numbers – More pupils, more money; fewer pupils, less money. Most funding increases are per pupil, and if your numbers are projected to fall over the next few years, you could end up with less money, even if the government announces national funding increases. Birth rates for your catchment area should be available from the local health authority via your local authority, but you will need to think about the trends in out-of-catchment applications. You will also need to think about the effect of any new house building or demolition in your area.

■ Rates of grant and start or finish dates for different projects or sources of funding – Many schools obtain time-limited grant funding and do not always take the loss of that grant into account in their future plans.

■ Known changes in income and expenditure – It should be possible to predict most changes, such as teachers moving up the pay scale (known as incremental drift). However, some changes, such as the introduction of Teaching and Learning Responsibility points (TLRs) and the introduction of Planning, Preparation and Assessment time (PPA) may be difficult to calculate and you might need to seek technical help.

■ Legislative changes (such as Workforce Reform) – This is perhaps the most difficult area of all, and you might may even ask whether long-term planning is practicable. Certainly, as we have mentioned, long-term planning is an inexact science. You should model different scenarios to allow for several possible outcomes.

■ External factors – This is where the assumptions established in the PESTE analysis in Chapter 1 can be used. If something is likely to happen because of external factors (such as a short-term influx of pupils, demolition of a housing estate, the end of a grant), this is the place to ensure that specific assumptions are allowed for.

Step 3: Understanding your financial position

Having agreed your planning assumptions, you can now make use of the stocktaking you did in Chapter 1, to get a thorough understanding of your current financial position.

Benchmarking

> Tip – Benchmarking your income and expenditure against other similar schools is an effective way of identifying possible problem areas in your financial plans.

We have already suggested that you use local benchmarking information as part of your initial stocktaking exercise. The purpose of benchmarking is comparing your income and expenditure against other similar schools to provide you with data on how effectively you are using your resources. For example, you can compare how much you are spending per pupil on say building maintenance compared with such schools. The main advantage of local benchmarking is that you can usually identify the schools you are comparing your school against and even contact the headteacher to compare notes.

However, there is also the national benchmarking website, which is fed by the financial information produced by schools in the format of the Consistent Financial Reporting Framework (CFR). The data are taken from the last financial year, collected by the DfES in a common format for all English and Welsh schools. Comparisons can be made with previous years. Your own CFR data will be automatically input from DfES records. You can select a number and range of national similar schools for comparison.

You will need to choose some of the criteria you can use to select the schools you wish to be compared with, for example, by:

■ number of pupils;

■ school phase and type;

■ type of establishment;

- urban or rural school;

- region;

- percentage eligible for free school meals;

- percentage of pupils with special educational needs (SEN) statements.

The schools in the sample you select (typically around 30) are anonymous, but you can email them through the website if you wish to make contact with them to seek further information.

Once you have selected a range of schools you will have access to a number of graphs. The data are presented in both cost per pupil and percentage ways and set out in CFR format. Figure 2.2 is an example of cost per pupil data for EO1, teaching staff.

As funding for schools varies from local authority to local authority, some argue that the percentage graphs are of more use. Of course, this information may raise more questions than answers, such as why do you spend 2 per cent more than the national average on teachers or £3 per pupil less than the national average on premises?

There may be a perfectly good reason why, but it may throw up issues that you simply had not considered. As FMSiS indicates (section 3.2), this should be discussed with the governing body. In fact, governors often find this information very useful, something that they can use to challenge how resources are being used. This reinforces their role of 'critical friend'.

Classroom organisation planning

Another important piece of analysis is to look at how you are utilising your teachers and classroom support staff. Some local authorities have software to help you with this and to consider the financial consequences. An example is shown in Figure 2.3.

It is particularly useful to work out pupil–teacher ratios (PTRs). You can calculate this by dividing the total number of pupils by the number of teaching staff including the headteacher. You could compare your PTRs with other schools, or look at the trend in your school over the last few years. You may find that your teaching workforce has remained broadly the same, while your pupil numbers have steadily decreased. Since most

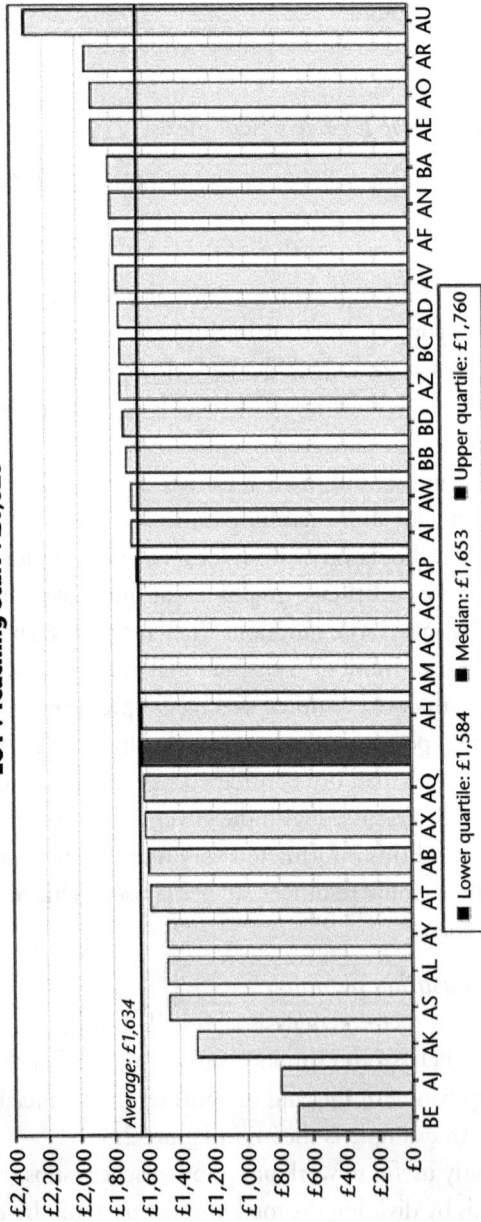

EO1 : Teaching Staff : £1,626

Average: £1,634

■ Lower quartile: £1,584 ■ Median: £1,653 ■ Upper quartile: £1,760

Figure 2.2 Cost per pupil for EO1, teaching staff

CLASSROOM ORGANISATION PLAN

CLASS ORGANISATION (Reception to Year 6)					FORECAST JANUARY PUPIL NUMBERS (EXCLUDING PUPILS IN IRU's)								
Class Name	Staff Name	Post	FTE	Key Stage	Reception	Year 1	Year 2	Year 3	Year 4	Year 5	Year 6	Total	Key Stage Total
					30	30	27	37	22	27	31	204	
	P.Smith	Teacher	1.00	F	30							30	
				F								0	
				F								0	30
	R.Richards	Teacher	1.00	KS1		30						30	
	J.Clark	Teacher		KS1								0	
	D.Bone	Teacher	1.00	KS1			27					27	
				KS1								0	
				KS1								0	
				KS1								0	57
	N.Harris	Teacher	1.00	KS2				18	11			29	
	M.Peters	Teacher	1.00	KS2				19	11			30	
	H.Taylor	Teacher	1.00	KS2								0	
	W.Chapman	Teacher	1.00	KS2							31	31	
	M.Corbett	Teacher	1.00	KS2						27		27	
				KS2								0	
				KS2								0	
				KS2								0	
Total			7.00		30	30	27	37	22	27	31	204	117

Figure 2.3 A classroom organisation plan

of your funding will be based on the number of pupils you have declared in your PLASC return, it is doubtful whether this can be sustained.

Step 4: Building a financial plan

Building your plan is really just bringing together all the information you have assembled, including, for example, the assumptions, and considering each element of the plan in turn. You can use the CFR (see Table 1.2 for a definition) as a tool for organising your information.

Although it is possible (just!) to build a financial plan on the back of an envelope, there are some very good spreadsheet tools around that can be used to save a lot of the hard work. If you are planning to model different scenarios, then a tool is really a necessity. Some local authorities provide tools as part of their subscription service; inevitably these vary in quality and functionality. There are also commercially available tools.

Tip – A good financial planning tool will help you plan a one-year budget and multiple years at the same time. It should be easy to use, require little specialist knowledge, be formatted along the lines of the CFR, and calculate the cost of salaries.

It is vital to involve stakeholders in the building of the plan. The administrator will advise the school leadership team, and conclusions should be presented to governors. Stakeholders should be fully aware of the outcomes of the plan and committed to the proposed actions.

Reporting the plan
Ideally, you should be able to present the conclusions of the plan in a lively and graphical format (a good financial tool will be able to help you do this). You should also save different versions of the plan to reflect possible future scenarios. The future is uncertain and your assumptions will need to model this. A typical example of how outcomes can be shown in tabular form is shown in Figure 2.4.

Green Valley Primary				
Summary Income and Expenditure Report				

2005/06		2006/07	2007/08	2008/09
	-	Balance at start of year	25,098	29,234	10,666
	-	Total Income	843,890	846,665	851,232
	-	Total Expenditure	839,754	865,233	903,445
	-	In Year Movement	4,136	- 18,568	- 52,213
	-	Balance at end of year	29,234	10,666	- 41,547

Figure 2.4 Summary income and expenditure report

In the example in Figure 2.4:

■ The *Balance at the start of the year* is the surplus or deficit brought from previous year.

■ *Total Income* is the total planned amount of funds made available to the school for each of the three years shown.

■ *Total Expenditure* is the planned expenditure for each of the three years shown.

■ *In Year Movement* is the difference (surplus or deficit) between income and expenditure within each of the three years shown.

■ The *Balance at the end of the year* is the surplus or deficit carried forward into the following year.

Figures 2.5 and 2.6 show the same information in graph form (very much easier to understand). Figure 2.6 demonstrates clearly, provided the assumptions are correct, that the school concerned is heading for a major deficit by 2008–09. It would be vital for this school to take action immediately to remedy the situation.

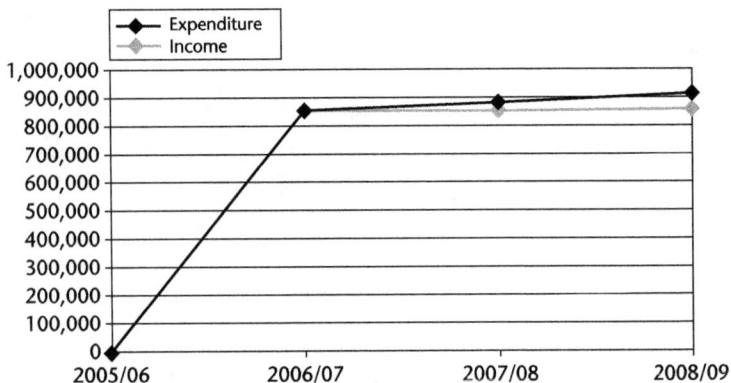

Figure 2.5 Income and expenditure graph

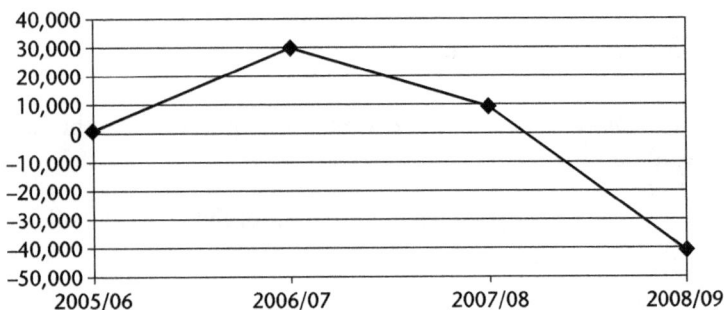

Figure 2.6 Surplus and deficit graph

Step 5: Using the financial plan

If the plan throws up major issues for the school it could be worth getting an independent person to check your assumptions. If you do have a possible substantial future deficit, you need to avoid unnecessary panic. It will be difficult enough to communicate difficult decisions to the governors, staff and parents without having to backtrack later. Schools have been known to make staff redundant and then find out that their decisions were based on incorrect assumptions. Even if your plan looks balanced for the next few years, there is no harm in checking that you haven't missed something important.

Once this independent check is done and the position is confirmed, you need to communicate it to governors and staff. If fewer staff are required you might want to get advice from a human resources specialist. Redundancy procedures are long and complex and there may be less painful alternatives such as early retirement or reduced staff working hours. One benefit of multi-year planning is that it can show up issues like this before action has to be taken.

You may also need to take short-term action to control expenditure, perhaps by putting a stop on spending in supply and/or equipment budgets. However, if you do this, keep your eyes firmly focused on the objectives of the school. You may wish to protect the English budget if you are trying to improve key stage 3 literacy results. Likewise, if there are significant health and safety issues with the building, particularly if they carry a risk to pupils, you may need to earmark money for repairs.

You should be able to model different solutions in your planning tool and work out options to resolve your difficulties. This will lead in nicely to work on your annual budget, which we will explore in Chapter 3.

Chapter 3

Annual budgets

It's clearly a budget. It's got a lot of numbers in it.

(George W. Bush)

Lots of numbers

The annual budget may well contain a lot of numbers but it is also a key tool in managing the resources available to your school. The annual budget serves a number of purposes:

- it shows how resources are to be allocated during the year to achieve your school's objectives;

- it provides a basis for monitoring and controlling spending;

- it demonstrates that the school's plans for the year are affordable.

In some cases the budget may show that the school's plans are not affordable and that budgeted expenditure during the year exceeds the expected income. A school with an in-year deficit such as this may be able to balance its budget in the short term by using surplus balances carried forward from the previous year. However, balances can only be used once and if the in-year deficit recurs in future years the school will very quickly find itself in serious financial difficulties.

The school governing body should approve the annual budget; schools are required to set a balanced budget. If a school cannot set a balanced budget, it may apply to its local authority for a 'licensed deficit' arrangement. This allows the school more than one year in which to balance their budget and usually requires the school to prepare and implement a recovery plan describing the actions that will be taken to balance the budget over the period of the agreement (normally two years).

Tip – A useful source of information about budget and other financial arrangements between a school and its local authority can be found in the Scheme for Financing Schools. Every authority is required to produce a scheme that sets out the local financial arrangements and regulations that the school and local authority will follow.

Long-term planning

The annual budget is a one-year budget covering the 12 months from 1 April each year. Uncertainty about future funding has meant that many schools do not look at the annual budget until advised by their local authority of the school's formula budget share in March just a few weeks before the start of the financial year. This has led to some schools planning their finances for a 12-month period rather than over a longer period.

Schools following a multi-year budgeting process would do much of the preparation for producing an annual school budget at a much earlier stage, usually in the autumn term prior to the beginning of the budget year. Following a longer-term planning approach described in Chapter 2 gives the school the opportunity to model estimated expenditure levels and therefore the approximate income requirements for the forthcoming year. When the actual funding is known in March the estimated income and expenditure requirements for the first year of the multi-year budget plan are reviewed and used as the basis for setting the annual budget.

The budgeting process

Whatever process schools use to determine their budget, whether as part of a multi-year planning process or a stand-alone annual budget process, the principles for building up the budget are the same. It is important to remember that the budget will be used as a monitoring tool to help the school manage its resources. A realistic budget will

- not build in unachievable income targets or unrealistic expenditure budgets – this will only result in a shortfall in income or an overspend on expenditure;

- reflect the cost of maintaining current levels of activity in the school;

- plan for the cost of any SDP activities that are to be implemented during the year;

- be affordable within the school's estimate of its income for the year.

Tip – It is important to remember that where a school has a surplus balance brought forward from the previous year this should be used to fund one-off expenditure only. If it is used to fund recurring costs (such as permanent staff) there will be no income to fund this expenditure in future years, when the surplus has been spent.

Formats

A budget should be set for each element of income and expenditure and for consistency and ought to be presented in a format that matches the DfES CFR. Many authorities provide their schools with an annual budget or multi-year planning spreadsheet in CFR format as a tool to help in the budget building process. There is also a number of commercial spreadsheets that are available to schools that provide the same functionality. Figure 3.1 is an example of a school's revenue budget in CFR format.

SUMMARY REVENUE BUDGET REPORT 2006/07

£

Revenue income

I01	Funds delegated by the local authority	928,100
I02	Funding for 6th form students –	
I03	SEN funding	47,500
I04	Funding for minority ethnic pupils –	
I05	Standards fund	37,100
I06	Other government grants –	
I07	Other grants and payments received –	
I08	Income from facilities and services	4,000
I09	Income from catering –	
I10	Receipts from supply teacher insurance claims –	
I11	Receipts from other insurance claims –	
I12	Income from contributions –	
I13	Donations and/or private funds –	
I14	School standards grant	44,700
I15	Funding for extended schools –	
I16	Income from extended school facilities –	
I17	Community focused extended school facilities –	
Total Revenue Income		1,061,400

Revenue expenditure

E01	Teaching staff	676,900
E02	Supply teaching staff	36,000
E03	Education support staff	114,500
E04	Premises staff	42,400
E05	Administrative and clerical staff	40,200
E06	Catering staff –	
E07	Cost of other staff	21,000
E08	Indirect employee expenses	3,000
E09	Staff development and training	5,500
E10	Supply teacher insurance 1	6,600
E11	Staff related insurance	3,200
E12	Building maintenance and improvement	7,500
E13	Grounds maintenance and improvement	4,000
E14	Cleaning and caretaking	3,100

(*continued*)

E15	Water and sewerage	5,900
E16	Energy	26,900
E17	Rates	11,900
E18	Other occupation costs	7,100
E19	Learning resources	38,200
E20	ICT learning resources	24,500
E21	Exam fees –	
E22	Administrative supplies	5,700
E23	Other insurance premiums	10,000
E24	Special facilities –	
E25	Catering supplies	12,200
E26	Agency supply staff –	
E27	Bought in professional services – curriculum	5,800
E28	Bought in services – other	10,000
E29	Loan interest –	
E30	Direct revenue funding –	
E31	Extended schools costs –	
E32	Extended schools staff –	
	Total Revenue Expenditure	1,132,100
	Revenue balance at the start of the year	72,200
	In-year balance –	70,700
	Revenue balance at the end of the year	1,500

Figure 3.1 Example of a school budget in the CFR format

Guidelines

When you begin to build up a budget for your school you may find it helpful to consider the following basic guidelines:

■ Establish a budget for each element of school income and expenditure, the level of detail should be consistent with the level of detail at which you intend to monitor and control actual income and expenditure.

■ Try to build each budget up from scratch, justifying every item that you include in the budget.

- Consider what is needed to maintain the school's existing provision as well as deliver SDP priorities during the year.

- Check that your budgeted spending is affordable – is your estimated income enough to cover your estimated expenditure? If not, review your budgets. Are there less expensive options for delivering the school's priorities? Are there cost savings or efficiencies that can be made? Are there options for additional income generation? Can any spending be deferred? Have charging and lettings policies been reviewed? Have service contracts been reviewed?

- Keep detailed working papers to show how the budget figures have been calculated.

- Include details of any assumptions you made when estimating income and expenditure.

Approaches

Zero-based budgeting
Building a budget from scratch is known as zero-based budgeting. The basic premise of zero-based budgeting is that no costs or activities should be automatically built in to the budget just because they were included in previous years.

The benefit this approach provides is the opportunity to systematically review your school's spending, looking at alternatives, reprioritising and perhaps withdrawing from long-term activities that no longer align properly with the school's objectives. However, it can be more time-consuming than incremental budgeting.

Incremental budgeting
Building up a budget using the previous year's figures as the base is known as incremental budgeting. The focus of the process is to identify and adjust for any anticipated changes from last year's figures such as inflation, full year effects, new developments, and so on.

This approach is easy to implement. However, the main danger of using an incremental approach is that you can very quickly lose sight of what is included in the base. The impact of historical decisions on the budget may be rolled forward without any challenge to the current appropriateness of those historic decisions.

The approach you use will usually be determined by the type of income and expenditure budget you are looking at. Where income or expenditure is of an ad hoc, unplanned and haphazard nature (such as day-to-day repairs), an incremental approach is the most suitable approach; previous years' spending is likely to be the best indicator of the level of spending you may need to incur. For items of income and expenditure that are of a predictable, planned and regular nature, a zero-based approach is recommended; it is a more robust and transparent method.

Expenditure

Staffing

Salary costs are usually between 75 to 80 per cent of a school's expenditure. It is therefore very important that the budget for staffing costs is detailed and accurate. Most budgeting spreadsheets available to schools include a facility that allows you to calculate your school's salary costs using a built-in salary calculator. If you do not have access to this type of spreadsheet, a teachers' pay calculator can be found on the Teachernet website.

When building a staffing budget:

- Try using a zero-based approach – start from scratch and justify why you need to include each staffing post in the budget.

- Reflect the estimated staffing costs required to deliver the new academic year curriculum plan and other SDP priorities.

- Use your school payroll information to check that staff are budgeted for on the correct grade, at the correct full- or part-time equivalent, and that you have included any additional allowances or overtime that may be payable.

- Remember to build in any annual increments that staff will receive.

- Build in new and vacant posts from the estimated date of appointment or date the post is to be filled.

■ Include the estimated cost of pay awards, with effect from the due date.

■ Include the cost of employers' National Insurance and superannuation contributions in the budget.

> Tip – If you are using a staffing calculator or budget spreadsheet then information on pay awards, National Insurance and superannuation rates should be built into the software and the costs automatically calculated. If you are not using such a tool then the information should be obtainable from your local authority's school finance or human resources sections. A search of the Internet will also provide several websites with the appropriate information. As a rule of thumb, you should currently add about 22% for superannuation and National Insurance for teachers. Support staff percentages will vary locally.

Building repairs and maintenance

Schools are responsible for repairs and maintenance and capital improvements to their buildings.

Capital improvements are funded from the devolved formula capital grant, which is allocated via local authorities direct to schools. You should try to prioritise spending on capital improvements in line with the school's longer-term responsibilities, preferably developing a Strategic Asset Management Plan for the school that aligns with the local authority's Asset Management Plans. Make sure that capital income and expenditure budgets are recorded separately from revenue income and expenditure budgets in the CFR. (Voluntary aided schools have slightly different arrangements.)

Revenue repairs and maintenance are funded through a school's delegated budget share. When setting your revenue repairs and maintenance budget, be sure to reflect the impact of any capital improvement spending you are planning to do.

Revenue repairs tend to be ad hoc and unpredictable, as such it may be best to take an incremental approach using the previous year's budget as a base and adjusting for any known changes. Building maintenance however is generally predictable, this type of budget is ideal for a zero-based approach building the budget from scratch based on planned levels of maintenance activities. Examples of incremental and zero based approaches are shown below.

E12 BUILDING MAINTENANCE AND IMPROVEMENT

Repairs and maintenance

Health & safety – electrical testing	£1,500
Planned maintenance – improvements to the boys' toilets	£2,200
Adaptation of Classroom 3 for foreign languages (School Development Plan)	£200
Day-to-day repairs (previous year's actuals plus 2 per cent inflation)	£1,500
Total budget	£5,400

Figure 3.2   Example of a zero-based budget approach

E12 BUILDING MAINTENANCE AND IMPROVEMENT

Repairs and maintenance

Previous year's budget	£5,000
Less one-off expenditure in previous year – girls' toilets improvements –	£1,800
Add improvements to boys' toilets	£2,200
Adaptations to Classroom 3 for foreign language development	£200
Total Budget	£5,600

Figure 3.3   Example of an incremental budget approach

Figures 3.2 and 3.3 show different answers because the incremental approach has rolled the previous year's budget forward and not identified or adjusted for changes to the day-to-day repairs budget. Often schools are unaware of what was originally included in the previous year and do not adjust the base budget. This can lead to confusion and possible over- or under-budgeting. The zero-based approach should ensure that the budget reflects only what a school needs to spend in the year.

Tip – If you are unsure about what is capital spending and what is revenue repair and maintenance spending, check your local Scheme for Financing Schools. This should detail as an appendix to the scheme details of a school's capital and revenue responsibilities.

Energy

Varying weather conditions can affect the level of expenditure on energy costs making it difficult to estimate requirements with certainty. This should not be an excuse to ignore the control of energy expenditure, as conservation of energy should be part of a school's attempts to use its limited resources in the most efficient way.

Energy budgets should initially be built up by calculating current usage at current prices – use recent and reliable historical levels of spending. This base figure should then be adjusted for the following if applicable:

- buildings or rooms to be newly opened;

- energy savings from stricter controls;

- the effect of installing energy management systems;

- costs arising from any additional school lettings.

Supplies and services

These budgets are often set on an incremental basis using previous years' levels of expenditure as a base and without thoroughly reviewing spending priorities. Try and take a zero-based approach to setting budgets for learning resources, information and communication technology (ICT) equipment and materials, itemising as far as possible requirements for large purchases and leaving a residual global amount for the purchase of small items.

Many primary schools distribute some of the supplies budget out to curriculum co-ordinators to give them delegated freedom to achieve the goals set in the SDP. The way in which this is done varies from school to school, from a single decision by the headteacher, to a collective leadership team decision, to recommendations to governors. Some schools will ask the curriculum co-ordinators to submit written bids, a process described by one head as 'blood on the carpet'! However, this may better reflect this year's school priorities than a historical model. Usually a basic amount is kept back for common school purchases such as pens and paper.

Tip – If you do base a budget on the previous year's level of expenditure, remember to take out any non-recurring items of expenditure and add any planned development costs.

Printing, postage, stationery

Many of these costs can be difficult to predict and an incremental approach basing the budget on previous years' levels of spending may be a good starting point. Larger known costs should be itemised in the budget build up, for example if you print a school prospectus each year the costs are predictable and can be separately identified in the budget. Similarly if you lease or rent photocopying equipment these costs should be known and itemised in the budget build up.

Income

It is important to estimate the amount of income your school will receive so that you can ensure your spending plans are affordable and ensure all income due to the school is received.

A large proportion of income is passed to schools via the local authority in the form of formula budget share/DSG and other direct grants such as Standards Fund and the School Standards Grant. Read and check the information provided by your local authority, compare the current year's funding with your previous year's funding so that you are aware of any significant changes. If you are unsure or don't understand how the funding has been calculated contact your local authority's finance department, in our experience they are usually very keen to help and give advice to schools.

You should budget for all sources of income that you expect the school to receive; often the income is related to expenditure you will be incurring. It is important that you budget for both the expenditure you will incur and the income you expect to receive. For example if you are letting out the school for sports and other activities, your expenditure budgets should include the cost of providing the lets and your income budgets should show the amount of money you expect to receive from those lets.

You can build income budgets in much the same way as expenditure budgets either on an incremental basis or from a zero base. If the income is predictable use a zero-based approach, if it is unpredictable take an incremental approach using previous year's income as a base. Of course, it is important to check that all this income will still follow through to the new financial year.

Typical sources of income are:

- lettings;

- class sales;

- income from catering;

- insurance claims;

- bank interest;

- donations and contributions.

Having completed your income and expenditure budgets you should then check that your estimated expenditure does not exceed your expected income. If it does you will need to review your income and expenditure to identify where expenditure can be reduced or income increased in order to achieve a balanced budget.

Recovery planning

If a school has got into serious financial difficulty and is unable to set a balanced budget then it needs to plan for how it will achieve a balanced budget over a longer period than a year. A school in this position will usually have to seek a 'licensed deficit arrangement' from its local authority. This arrangement allows schools to set a deficit budget providing they have clear plans for balancing the budget over a period of time, which is agreed with the local authority.

Most local authorities will require plans from the school showing how they intend to balance their budget and will monitor the school to ensure that the proposed recovery actions are undertaken. Schools may be required to provide the authority with more frequent financial monitoring information, in extreme circumstances where schools fail to take appropriate action the local authority may suspend the school's delegated financial powers.

There are three basic steps for a recovery plan if your school is in financial difficulty:

- acknowledge the problem;
- analyse your current year's budget;
- consider your options.

Acknowledge the problem
All stakeholders need to recognise and understand that there is a problem.

Analyse your current year's budget
Get a detailed and accurate understanding of the current budget position:

- Identify staffing structures and costs.
- Identify where the resources go.
- Benchmark to compare levels of spending.
- Analyse income streams; is all income included?
- Are financial controls and monitoring processes effective?

Consider your options
Consider the options for additional income generation and the achievement of cost savings over both the short and long term:

- Identify recurrent and non-recurrent income and cost savings.

■ Use benchmarking information to identify areas of high spend and review them.

■ Review your SDP – Can any planned spending be deferred, such as classroom adaptations or painting programmes? Can changes be made to number and mix of staff, such as having mixed-age classes or using teaching assistants?

■ Review working practices – Can you collaborate with other schools or agencies?

■ Review income sources – Are there new sources of grant income that could be bid for?

■ Does your charging and lettings policy need reviewing? Are there opportunities for income generation or commercial sponsorship?

The purpose of a recovery plan is to identify the actions that can be taken to bring your school budget back in to a balanced position within an agreed period of time. The plan can be a simple statement showing:

■ what actions will be taken;

■ when the actions will happen;

■ how much will be saved by taking the action.

The actions should be an outcome from the review and consideration of options from the work detailed above.

Chapter 4
Checking progress

*All decent people live beyond their incomes nowadays, and those who
aren't respectable live beyond other peoples. A few gifted individuals
manage to do both.*

(Saki, *The Chronicles of Clovis*)

Most schools channel a lot of energy into setting the budget as we have
discussed in Chapters 2 and 3 but this is not where it ends. In setting a
budget the school has worked out what it plans to do over the coming
months and years, but how will you determine if these ideas were
turned into actions and whether the costs and timings were as you
planned?

The answer lies in how you control the systems that the school uses
and then how you monitor the school's financial performance. It is all
too easy to conclude that this no more than checking how much
money you have left at various times of the year, but is this all you
need to know?

There are four steps in the checking process:

- review and monitor internal control systems;

- review and monitor budgets;

- control actions;

- make improvements.

Review and monitor internal control systems

In order to work out what you control, it might first be helpful to look at your responsibilities, which can be summarised as follows:

■ Carry out your delegated authority as agreed by the governing body.

■ Define the roles and responsibilities of your staff.

■ Comply with the local authorities' financial regulations and standing orders.

■ Ensure that systems of internal control are in place.

Delegated authority is a term that sounds grand but really just describes the day-to-day responsibilities that you have, this will include the parameters within which you can spend the school's money, whether it is for pencils or to meet your strategic plans such as those in Chapter 2.

One of the above responsibilities is to ensure that systems of internal control are in place, but what are these internal controls?

■ Internal checks – one person checking another person's work.

■ Separation of duties – no one member of staff having responsibility for a whole process.

■ Systems of authorisation – each transaction is authorised before it is taken forward.

■ System manuals – descriptions of how systems work, who does what and when.

■ Audit trail – practice of being able to follow an order through from delivery note to invoice and vice versa.

You will need to ensure that the processes and systems that are in place for things such as ordering, payments, payroll, income etc. are clearly defined and documented, incorporating the five elements of internal control. This can be particularly useful when key staff are off for long periods of time as it enables other people to pick up their duties.

The above elements will also be reviewed when the school self-evaluates its progress against the Financial Management standard that has been defined by the DfES and through the work that internal audit will carry out in your school.

So this now begs a question, that if it's not good enough to simply say that you do something, how will you be able to demonstrate that you have the appropriate controls in place and that they work?

While your time needs to be split between educational outcomes and the welfare of staff and pupils, you also need to give priority to financial controls. We have all read in the papers cases where internal controls were weak or simply not applied and then the headteacher has been called to account. In most cases this has resulted in the school spending beyond its means, on inappropriate items, or even in cases of public fraud. So what can you do to prevent this?

- Get systems and processes documented.

- Check for yourself that things are working correctly.

- Review with staff how things work and where problems often occur.

- Ask key questions before committing the school to activities, such as 'have we got the budget to pay for this, do we need it?'.

- Review a sample of transactions that have taken place.

All of these methods will give you some insight into how things are working or not working as the case may be.

Of course this could all be seen as shutting the stable door after the horse has bolted, therefore the best method of ensuring control is to be clear with staff what their roles and responsibilities are and how things work in your school, and this should be defined in a finance policy.

Many local authorities will have a model policy, as does the FMSiS Toolkit (R16) that you will need to tailor to your specific requirements. The policy would define all the key arrangements such as:

- Delegated authority (clarity on the spending powers of full governors, finance committee, headteacher).

- How this should be evidenced (minuted, signed for).

- Operation of key systems and processes (insurance, petty cash, ordering).

- Reporting arrangements (who reports are provided to and how often).

Your local authority will have laid down financial regulations that all schools must comply with; these may include purchasing arrangements, for example at what point the school will need to enter formal tendering arrangements. Equally the way that staff conduct themselves, including when and how they need to disclose any relationships with third-party providers.

Tip – If you are unsure about purchasing arrangements or the registering of business interests check your local Scheme for Financing Schools or alternatively you could check the DfES Purchasing Guide (R36) in FMSiS.

Review and monitor budgets

While we said earlier that monitoring may be as simple as just checking how much money was left, it might be worth considering what you need to check up on and how often you would need to do this. Thinking back to the earlier chapters you should review your:

- strategic plans;

- assumptions;

- actual income and expenditure;

- cash flow.

The frequency of review will depend on the circumstances that the school finds itself in. It would be appropriate to review your strategic plans and planning assumptions on a termly basis. Income and expenditure and the school's cash flow should be monitored more frequently on a monthly/quarterly cycle. If the school, however, has a deficit budget then these reviews may need to be completed on a monthly basis.

Having identified the costs associated with your strategic plans in Chapter 2 you should be considering if your plans have developed at the pace and cost that you anticipated. What normally happens is that you will take opportunities as they arise which may not always match exactly what your strategies were at the start of the year. Health and safety work is a classic example: at the start of the year you will have had a plan of what work needed to be completed, however during the year other priorities will arise that need to be dealt with. If the school has been vandalised over the weekend and a number of windows have been damaged the school would need to make these safe regardless of whether you had budgeted to do this or not. Likewise, an unsatisfactory fire drill may lead you to conclude that you need extra resources for fire equipment or improved exit controls on doors.

Equally the assumptions that you made in the budget may be different in reality to those that you predicted. This may be due to changes in government policy, parental preference or school priorities. Given that this will happen, what you need to consider is how you will deal with it. Will you:

- React immediately and update all your plans?
- Contemplate why things were different?
- Ignore the differences and just carry on?

In reality you will probably apply all three strategies at some time as it often depends on the significance of the change. The common factor with all three is that you will have to communicate with governors what action should be taken.

Actual income and expenditure

Income and expenditure budgets will have been set at the start of the year, based on what you thought would happen. The information in your financial management system will need to reflect these levels of budget so that you are able to monitor actual income that you receive and payments that you make during the year.

Table 4.1 was based on information at the end of August. It is unclear whether the actual figures reflect where you thought you would be at this point in the year. To enhance this information further you need to think about which months you expect things to happen in. If we look at the same position again but add a bit more detail it might become clearer.

Table 4.1   Example of a budget showing actual expenditure

Description	Annual budget	Actual	Difference
	£	£	£
Repairs and maintenance	20,000	8,000	12,000
Learning resources	10,000	7,000	3,000

Table 4.2 now shows the information slightly differently, this is because we are comparing the actual position with where we thought that we would be. In the example we have only spent £8,000 of the repairs and maintenance budget but we had planned to spend £13,000. This is because important and expensive summer repairs to the roof were planned. You should then be asking why haven't we spent the £13,000. Is it that:

■ The work hasn't been completed?

■ The work has been completed but we haven't had an invoice?

Table 4.2   Example of actual expenditure and anticipated expenditure

Description	Annual budget	Anticipated budget to date	Actual	Difference
	£	£	£	£
Repairs and maintenance	20,000	13,000	8,000	5,000
Learning resources	10,000	6,000	7,000	−1,000

■   The work wasn't as expensive as you thought?

■   Due to sub-standard work the school has not released all the money?

With learning resources we have spent more money than we expected. Is it because:

■   Unplanned items have been bought?

■   The cost of items has risen?

You need to obtain the right information from your systems to make informed decisions.

Reports

There are two types of report that you can prepare for governors:

■   income and expenditure;

■   year-end forecast.

Income and expenditure reports show whether the school's income and expenditure levels are where you expected them to be. If they are not then you will need to investigate the reasons why and suggest corrective action.

The advantages are that this approach is easy to complete and simple to understand. However, future commitments are not included and may have a significant impact on the financial position of the school in later months.

Year-end forecast reports build on information in the income and expenditure report (such as level of budget, actual income and expenditure to date) and include a prediction of what will happen for the remainder of the year. In general, you have to decide whether the way that you have received income and made payments in the first part of the year will continue as a trend. If not, then you will have to work out why and determine what may happen.

This approach can be more informative for governors as it identifies the likely year-end position. Early decisions can then be taken if needed to reprioritise the use of resources or reduce the planned spending of the school. However, to complete a year-end forecast properly will take time and this approach is still susceptible to the occurrence of unforeseen events.

Many local authorities and some private companies can help you with software and advice to help you construct reports that will meet your needs and those of your governors.

Don't panic!

When you take your first look at your monitoring reports you may be tempted to panic if the figures look worse than you expected. Keep calm and think carefully about what may be behind these figures. If you have spent 70 per cent of the repairs and maintenance budget in the first six months that may not necessarily mean that you are in financial difficulty. It could just be that you have timetabled most of the work for the summer holidays.

However, if you have spent 70 per cent of the gas budget by September, you could have serious problems. You may need to find ways of reducing spending to make up for the deficiency. You might have to cut back on planned equipment purchase or the supply budget to make up the difference. Once you have established that there is a genuine overspend (or shortfall in income), whatever you do, do not ignore it. The sooner you take action the more likely you are to be able to make the savings you need. Don't rely on someone else to sort it out for you.

Beware also the unexpected surplus. In some respects it is more risky than a deficit. Ask yourself if it is real. Don't spend the extra money until you are sure it really exists. Is there a bill waiting to be paid you have forgotten about? Are you sure that the summer fête is going to bring in the income you expect? Suppose it rains?!

Control actions

So far we have put the controls in place and thought about what we need to check on, but the final stage is probably the most important. There are two steps left:

■ How we explain the position to governors.

■ What corrective actions we take.

Governors will have been involved in setting plans at the start of the year but you will have to consider how you keep them updated of any significant changes or developments.

Tip – Simplicity in reports is the best option – use words to describe the financial position rather than lots of numbers.

Many heads take the easy option and pass around a copy of the reports from their financial information system with no explanation of what the information means. It is worth establishing with the governing body or finance committee what type of information they would like and offer some training to help them with the role.

Some apparently well-informed governors (even an odd accountant or two) might think that they understand accounts, but be unfamiliar with public sector ones. Very likely, they will need some assistance as to what is material in the accounts. Discourage them from devoting hours to the £5 overspend on the telephone bill, and point them towards the £100k underspend on salaries.

When you report to governors this will be to explain that

1   everything is on track; or

2   something has happened that alters the position; or

3   you could change strategies now, which will alter the position.

Often you will find that your explanations are around options 1 and 2, where you are trying to explain things that have happened. These can be difficult sessions. The more dynamic governor sessions tend to be around option 3, where you are giving them the option to shape what will happen. In reality this approach is merely an extension of the budget-setting process.

Tip – *Always* go into governor meetings with ideas for a way forward. Be prepared to discuss and debate – but never go in 'naked'!

Governors will expect you to advise them of risk areas that could put the school budget under pressure and ways to reduce the risk. Pressure may come from two sources. The school either has immediate problems or will be facing problems by the end of the year. Whatever the case, you will have to explain how the position arose and what you are going to do about it. You will probably need to examine the over- and underspends in some detail.

Did the overspend result from:

- A breakdown in internal controls?
- Items of expenditure (that could be deferred until next year)?
- A miscoding of income and expenditure?

If you have an overspend, you may want to think about putting a stop on expenditure or generating extra income. Did the underspend result from:

- A key project not taking place?
- A miscoding of income and expenditure?

As headteacher you should be mainly concerned with the overall position of the school's finances. Once you are satisfied on this point you can drill down into areas of income and expenditure to see where the problems may be.

Tip – Highlight the five most significant points in a report. This will keep you from getting bogged down in lots of detail.

Make improvements

Once a problem has been identified by you or an external assessor then you will need to decide how you intend to prevent this happening again.

If the problem relates to the systems of internal control you should consider whether the act was a deliberate one for someone's personal benefit, or simply a breakdown in the process that the school was using. Either way, the fact that this happened in both examples identifies a problem with the systems.

Where you identify that a problems exists, you will need to investigate the potential impact of the breakdown in the system. If you are unable to do this then you should contact your internal audit team for advice or assistance.

Where there is evidence that staff have tried to defraud the school, this should be dealt with through your human resources team; in some circumstances you may be advised to contact the police. It may raise concerns for you about the number of people involved in a process or the checking arrangements that are in place. If the fraud is related to money then you will have to decide with human resources if this person can be trusted with financial transactions in the future or if they might need to face disciplinary action.

We started this chapter by reviewing your key responsibilities and one of those related to you ensuring that systems of internal control were in place. If these systems are not adequate then it is up to you to make improvements.

Once you and the governors have reviewed the financial position and discussed the reasons why things either did or did not occur then you need to decide what to do. We have said that simplicity is often the best option and many believe that once you have set a budget, it should not be altered. If this is the case for your school, you would simply report on the discrepancy for the remainder of the year.

Alternatively, you could move money between budget heads. For example you may decide that the school needs to spend more than its budget for textbooks; what you will have to decide is where this money will come from. The one drawback with this method is that it complicates the budget-setting process in future years. In general the main reason why people revise the budget is because they have failed to control the costs throughout the year.

You will have to consult with governors on whether the information that you provide is sufficient, clear, timely and helpful. From this discussion you will need to decide what alterations to make.

Chapter 5

Managing buildings

You have to give this much to the Luftwaffe: when it knocked down our buildings it did not replace them with anything more offensive than rubble. We did that.

(Prince Charles)

▨ Rubble!

In March 2006, the Secretary of State for Education announced proposals to rebuild or refurbish half of all primary schools by 2022, with £1.15 billion of investment. In her speech, she acknowledged that there were nearly 11,000 primary schools built between 1945 and 1976, and now at the end of their lives.

Many heads would accept that there has been considerable investment in school buildings in the last ten years, although the effect of this has not been uniform across all schools. Despite this investment, there is still a substantial national backlog of repairs and maintenance still to be addressed.

We have already stressed in Chapter 1 the importance of an Asset Management Plan and described how one can be assembled. Having done this, the next step is to find the funds to undertake the prioritised work.

Funding for premises work

Formula funding

Most schools receive their repairs money through the local authority as part of the formula-based share. How this is calculated will vary from authority to authority, many will simply base it on the square metre area of the school, which is often seen to be fairest. However, some authorities will use the Asset Management Plan to take into account the condition of the schools and prioritise those schools in the worst state. Others may also factor in the number of children using the school, whether the school is on a split site, how big the school field is, or even what altitude the school is at! More importantly, funds are often provided to match the site-specific issues such as the actual size of utility bills, or what heating the school has.

In reality, there are only three things you can do about the repairs and maintenance funding you receive:

- You may be able to persuade your cluster/pyramid group to press the Schools Forum to revise the formula.

- You may wish to check that the figures on which the formula allocation is based are correct. Sometimes, local authorities miscalculate the school floor area, or omit key costly features of the school, such as coal-fired central heating.

- You should definitely try to prioritise the premises funding for its specific purposes, and be cautious about using it to prop up (for example) the salaries budget. The local authority is unlikely to be sympathetic to applications for further funding if you have used premises funds for other purposes.

Devolved Formula Capital Grant (DFC)

DFC gives schools direct funding to help support the capital needs of their buildings. It is initially allocated to local education authorities that are then required to allocate the funding directly to schools using a simple formula. This formula for distribution varies slightly, but in general, schools will receive a lump sum and then a formula-based amount per pupil numbers. Some local authorities distribute it at the beginning of the financial year, others have agreed with schools to hold it centrally for schools to access when required. DFC can be saved up over a three-year maximum period to accrue enough for a major scheme of work. However, local authorities must ensure that the total available schools pot is not exceeded in any one year.

DFC is available for construction works of a high value and long life, rather than for day-to-day repairs. It should be invested in the priorities agreed locally and identified in the local Asset Management Plan. Voluntary aided schools will find that the rules are slightly different as funds are distributed through the diocese.

Examples of what schools might use DFC for include:

- new roof structures;

- drainage in a new building/extension;

- providing a new covered link etc. between existing buildings;

- window framing – structural replacement programme;

- large-scale toilet refurbishment;

- kitchens in new buildings etc.

Local authorities will advise (through the Scheme for Financing Schools) on what should be financed by repairs funds and what by DFC.

Seed Challenge

Until 2004–05 schools could apply for central government funding to improve buildings 'to increase pupil achievement'. This money was again not to be used for general maintenance or for routine repairs, but rather for capital projects. Primary schools were expected to contribute 50 per cent of their own money to 'match fund' the project. Although the national scheme has ceased, the DfES encouraged local authorities to produce local schemes and a few have done so, based on similar arrangements.

Modernisation funding

This is DfES funding available to local authorities to assist in raising educational standards by contributing towards the capital investment needs of school buildings, according to locally agreed priorities identified in the Asset Management Plan. The distribution to local authorities is based on local need and pupil needs, but local authorities can obtain further funding through Targeted Capital funds.

Disability Discrimination Act (DDA)

The Schools Access Initiative (SAI) provides funding to make main-stream schools more accessible to children with disabilities, crucial now that the DDA makes it unlawful to discriminate against disabled pupils for a reason relating to their disability without justification. The SAI provides funding to make mainstream schools more accessible to children with disabilities and SEN by funding projects such as stair lifts, ramps, disabled toilets etc. See the Teachernet website for more information on this.

Private Finance Initiative (PFI)

Although PFI money has been prioritised towards secondary schools, and the Building Schools for the Future money is currently exclusive to the secondary sector, some primary schools have been rebuilt using PFI money, as have some through Special Schools. The main difference between a traditionally funded new school and a PFI school is that the building contractor leases back the building and continues to provide building services once the building is complete. So the contractor might arrange repairs, clean the building, deal with security and even provide catering. Contracts typically last 25 years, and governing bodies enter into an agreement with the local authority to use the premises related part of their delegated budget with the contractor to contribute to the cost of the arrangements.

Heads will be naturally attracted by the prospect of a new purpose-built school, and sharing the risk with a private contractor may also have its attractions. It also enables headteachers to focus on their core business of teaching and learning.

However, those who already have such schools might wish to draw attention to some disadvantages. Some heads have found the loss of control problematic; it clearly depends on the original contract and the performance of the contractor. If the contract is inflexibly written, it may not take account of changes in the number of pupils in a school, or whether parts of the school are under-utilised. Sometimes the sources of funding are insufficient to meet the required payments to the contractor and an affordability gap develops.

Local authorities have learned a great deal from the first PFI contracts and are closing up the loopholes in these contract specifications. Even so, some schools have suffered from extra running costs through contract variations not being sufficiently well specified in the contract. If you are entering into a PFI arrangement for a new school, you would be well advised to spend time ensuring that this work is properly described.

Choosing a contractor

Section 4.1 of the FMSiS gives excellent advice on the choice of a contractor, far more comprehensively than we can do here. This is linked to a very good Purchasing Guide for schools, published by the DfES. Essentially, however you will have the following choices when you need premises work undertaken.

Do-it-yourself

Many schools are asking their building staff to undertake basic repair jobs, and this is proving generally successful. However, you need to ensure that your staff are properly trained and have access to appropriate tools, and you should not carry out electrical or gas work unless your staff member is qualified. Some schools have used parent volunteers, but you need to check that they are also suitably trained, and insured. Be aware that if they do produce poor quality work you would not be able to sue them if you have not paid them. If they injure themselves or another person, you are likely to find that your insurance does not cover you when you are subject to a claim.

Small local contractors

More and more schools are choosing small local contractors, and they can provide excellent value for money. However, check that they have public liability insurance, are paying income tax, and have safe systems of working for the work to be carried out.

Local authority-approved contractors

These are probably better for larger premises contracts, and quite often basic checks have been undertaken before you approach them, including insurance and quality thresholds, health and safety policies and also financial soundness. Many contractors have gone bankrupt in the middle of school jobs, leaving work unfinished. Avoid money upfront for this reason. It is best to shop around for quotations; three is a typical number. Try to get references from work done with other schools.

Local authority in-house services

Some heads regard these as being expensive and slow, but they do usually provide a secure service, with few risks of the kind listed above.

Getting value for money

It is all too easy to focus on price as the only important factor in choosing a contractor. However, value for money is much broader than that, and the following is a list of other factors you should consider in awarding your contract for premises work:

- capacity and reputation of provider;
- quality of output;
- range of service provision;
- responsiveness;
- reliability;
- compatibility with the school ethos and culture.

Professional buyers will focus on these broader criteria, rather than just price. They often quote the acronym MEAT; that is the 'Most Economically Advantageous Tender'.

The following are the seven steps in the process for obtaining a contractor to undertake premises work, monitoring and reviewing their work, particularly on a large scale. The process may seem onerous but many heads have regretted not taking each step when a premises contract has gone wrong. When the contractor sets fire to your roof because the tar boiler is too near to the building on a windy day, you may wish that you had asked about and checked a safe system of working.

- Identify requirement and draft specification.

- Agree criteria to evaluate quotes.

- Source the market both internal and external.

- Issue a request for quotes or bids to the appropriate number of suppliers.

- Evaluate responses and select the one that is the most economically advantageous.

- Award and issue order to the successful supplier; debrief other unsuccessful suppliers.

- Manage delivery of goods and services.

Long-term contracts

Of course, some premises contracts are much longer term than (say) repairs to the school playground. Contracts for cleaning, school meals, electrical testing, and utilities can all last several years. For this reason, many primaries will ask their local authority to negotiate a deal on their behalf. This is sensible, as the collective buying power of many schools is likely to lead to a better deal than a single school. In the absence of such arrangements, groups of schools can combine together to improve their buying power. Do not be afraid to take, or even pay for, technical advice to assist with this process. It is unlikely that you have the knowledge and experience you need to undertake this kind of long-term contract. For example, to meet the legislative requirements for establishing a school kitchen, you would be well advised to seek some professional help.

Monitoring the school building

It is vital to set up a regular programme of servicing and testing to ensure that the school building is safe and unlikely to adversely affect staff or pupils. A record of such inspections should be kept, and organisations chosen to undertake statutory checks must be recognised by an appropriate industry standard. For example, CORGI registered gas fitters must be used to check gas boilers.

Table 5.1 lists things that must be checked and how frequently they should be checked. In addition to the statutory checks listed here it would be as well to set up a programme of building checks to review the need for maintenance and repairs. Typical examples are shown in Table 5.2.

Table 5.1 Statutory plant and equipment servicing and testing table

Servicing and testing	Frequency
Gas soundness testing	Annual
Oil and gas boilers	Quarterly/bi-annual/annual
Gas appliances	Gas safety check (every 11 months)
Chimneys/flues	Bi-annual/annual
Portable appliances testing	Annual for 'portable' equipment e.g. a soldering iron Twice yearly for double insulated or 'less portable' equipment e.g. a PC
Water quality sampling	Temperature – monthly Chlorination – annually
Gas catering equipment	Annual service
Portable fire fighting equipment	Annual service
Fixed electrical wiring installation	Five year test One year test where the installation is in poor condition – determine at service
Fire safety risk assessment	When any change occurs to the building

Table 5.2 An example of a set of maintenance checks

Elements	Maintence activity	Frequency
Window and door locks	Periodic inspection of lock and security	Weekly
Decoration	Periodic inspection – rolling programme of works	Annually
Water supply systems	Periodic inspection and ad hoc repairs	Annually
Lightning protection	Periodic inspection and ad hoc repairs	Every 11 months
Fixed sports and gymnasium equipment	Periodic inspection and ad hoc repairs	Every six months
Playgrounds	General inspection, maintenance and surface treatment	Regular recorded checks

Chapter 6
Managing health and safety

Out of this nettle, danger, we pluck this flower, safety.
(William Shakespeare, *Henry V, Part One*)

Grasping the nettle

No headteacher would say that health and safety is low priority.
However, this does not mean that health and safety is given appropriate
attention or risks are properly managed. Because accidents are rare and
are fortunately usually not serious, other priorities take precedence and
complacency all too easily creeps in. A school does not seem like a
particularly unsafe environment, not (say) compared with a factory or a
building site. But it is particularly risky to see health and safety as an
exclusively premises issue. It is a moral, legal and economic issue.
Taking care of health and safety is clearly 'the right thing' to do and as a
moral issue needs no discussion. But the legal and economic aspects of
health and safety deserve close attention.

Long-term risks

The consequences of ignoring risks may not come to light for many
years. For example, teachers can work at home on laptops for years
before shoulder, back or wrist problems develop. Just because the school
fishpond has never caused any difficulty, this does not mean that a year
one student will not fall in and drown.

Civil actions

Parents may choose to make claims against the school for an injury to their child many years after the incident. Unlike adults, who only have three years after an accident to make a claim, minors can make a claim up until three years after their eighteenth birthday. It has been known for such claims to be made up to ten years after the injury, and as long as medical records or signs of injury still exist, the claim may still be valid. Of course, in contrast school records may not exist after such a period and the relevant staff may have moved on. Even worse, claims are now being made for instances of bullying or lack of special needs help. Civil actions are usually against the local authority in community schools but could be against the governors in voluntary aided schools.

Accident books

With the compensation culture we live in, it is vital that you keep good records and one of the key tools for this task is the accident book. Take the writing up of even minor accidents seriously as you never know when it may be scrutinised later. It is understandably difficult to remember years later the actions you took, and you may need that record to demonstrate them. It is also good practice to carry out accident investigations to determine the root cause(s) of an accident, and to enable you to put measures into place to prevent a similar accident in the future.

Legislation and training

Not even a health and safety adviser could expect school staff to be conversant with all the relevant legislation, but the underlying principles can be straightforward and training should be provided for all staff during their induction, and then on specific subjects according to their individual role and responsibilities. Heads should also ensure that each member of staff is competent to carry out the tasks that are required of them.

Remember that health and safety legislation is criminal law and there could be prosecutions following breaches. These could be against individuals, the school including the head and governors, and the local authority.

Defect sheets

A useful practical tip is to pin up a defect sheet in each classroom, which collected on a weekly basis can provide useful information on low-level problems, which need to be resolved. Of course, if nothing is done about any of them, that might make matters still worse.

Safety governors

Much of what appears on the agenda of the governing body is fairly academic, and some governors appreciate being given practical tasks to undertake. You could ask a governor to take a special interest in health and safety matters; they might wish to accompany leadership team members on safety inspections and to report back to the governing body on issues arising.

What a health and safety policy should cover

We have already discussed responsibilities for this topic in Chapter 1, and it is vital for schools to have a 'site-specific' policy covering these responsibilities. Local authorities can often provide templates for this purpose, but it is crucial that they are properly adapted for the school, and then kept up to date. It is impossible to provide an exhaustive list of issues to be covered in such a policy but the following list should help:

- a general statement of policy;
- delegated roles and responsibilities;
- arrangements for carrying out the policy which may include the following:
    - staff training;
    - off-site visits;

- selecting and controlling contractors;
- first aid and supporting pupils' medical needs;
- school security;
- occupational health services and work-related stress;
- consultation arrangements with employees;
- workplace safety for teachers, pupils and visitors;
- violence towards staff;
- manual handling;
- slips and trips;
- on-site vehicle movements;
- management of asbestos;
- control of hazardous substances;
- maintenance of equipment;
- reporting of injuries, diseases and dangerous occurrences;
- recording of accidents;
- minibuses and transport;
- fire safety;
- dealing with emergencies.

In addition, some related policies such as bullying and attendance will have health and safety implications. Most local authorities can provide specific guidance on the above issues and additionally the Teachernet website contains useful guidance.

All staff should be acquainted with this policy, initially as part of their induction training and then on an ongoing basis according to circumstances arising. Governors should approve it and regularly review it.

Current key health and safety issues

Off-site visits and adventure activities

The popular press like to return to this topic on a regular basis, and it is hardly surprising that some schools/teachers have expressed some reluctance to continue with visits when they are the subject of this blame culture. Any mistake leading to death or injury is not easily forgiven, even when dangers have been extremely difficult to anticipate. There is a useful DfES document *Health and Safety of Pupils on Educational Visits* (HASPEV), which provides detailed information on planning a visit, and many local authorities add their own local guidance. It is essential to note that some trips carry their own special risks and plan accordingly. Examples would be foreign visits and farms. It is also important to be aware of the relevant legislative framework, particularly:

■ the Activity Centres (Young Persons' Safety) Act 1995;

■ the SEN and Disability Act 2001.

Teachers act in loco parentis for school trips. This means that they have a common law duty to take the same care that a reasonably prudent parent would take in similar circumstances. Under the Management of Health and Safety at Work Regulations 1999, the visit leader is required to make assessments of the risks to which employees, pupils and others are exposed in order that appropriate measures are taken to protect their health and safety. Leaders are also required to:

■ assess the risks of activities;

■ introduce measures to control those risks;

■ tell its employees about these measures.

Site security/violence to staff

Most schools will have taken action to improve site security over the last few years, especially with government money being available to provide such measures as CCTV, locks and perimeter fencing. It is all too easy to rely on technology for this purpose, and to overlook good processes. If a teacher leaves a door open, and a child wanders into the road and is knocked down by a vehicle, the best security in the world will not help. The consequences of such a tragic event, with all the local negative publicity and parental anger will affect everyone.

Many health and safety inspections will focus on this subject, not just on exits, but also of course on keeping out unwanted strangers. Attacks on staff are regrettably becoming more common, and you owe a duty of care to them to create and maintain effective site security.

ICT

We can all appreciate that electricity is dangerous, and that the wiring in the computer room needs checking, but the Display Screen Equipment Regulations of 1992 should also be adhered to. This requires individual assessments for employees to be carried out and documented. Vision screening may be required, paid for by the school. Employees need to take short regular breaks, and to have a variety of work to undertake. This is not usually a problem in the school office! What can be a problem is space in which to operate. All too often other staff intrude on the working space of school administrators and create workflow difficulties.

Fire safety

It is perhaps fortunate most school fires take place when the students are not in the building, often being started by intruders following break-ins. This is no excuse for being complacent about fire safety. Under the Regulatory Reform Order 2006, senior managers are responsible for ensuring that regular fire assessments are carried out and documented. Ideally this should happen each year, and be accompanied by practice evacuations and checking of fire equipment. Certain high-risk areas such as kitchens or boiler houses may require more frequent checks.

School kitchens

Schools are now starting to opt out of local authority contracts and are starting to set up their own catering arrangements, sometimes in co-operation with other schools. The legislation covering school kitchens is complicated, including food hygiene, and is not collected together into one easily accessible place. However, School Food Trust has a steadily improving website that is likely to provide such assistance in the medium term.

Reporting of Injuries, Diseases and Dangerous Occurrences Regulations (RIDDOR)

All accidents should be recorded on site, but the more serious accidents/injuries may be reportable under RIDDOR. If a serious accident takes place in the school, it should be reported to the Health and Safety Executive and the local authority's health and safety team.

Achieving effective health and safety

Throughout this book we have stressed the importance of effective management (and the overlap) of finance, premises and health and safety. To achieve this there must be clarity about roles, responsibilities and accountability. By developing a proactive approach for an effective health and safety culture, you will be complying with your statutory risk assessments, and obligations and duty of care.

Chapter 7

Reporting and getting help

A local government officer deals with the public, and with the public's money, and is in a real sense a trustee of that public money and (s)he must never allow his/her personal interest to come before the discharge of such duties.

(Cassidy v. Dorset C.C. . . . 1979)

Who you need to report to

Any member of the public has the right to look at the school accounts, because school budgets are public funds, and you are a public sector employee and therefore a trustee of those funds. Fortunately, few people actually take up this opportunity, although it is not unknown for individual parents to ask how funds are being used. For example, they might seek reassurance that sufficient special needs money is earmarked for the support of their child. Sometimes trade unions ask for information about allocation of funds when the school is making staffing cuts.

So far as finance is concerned, there are four stakeholders you need to report to:

■   parents;

■   governors;

■   the local authority;

■   the DfES.

Why you need to report to anyone

Some heads find it hard to understand why they have to report on their budget to anyone when the local authority has delegated that budgetary responsibility to them. Some of their governors may concur with this, arguing that this is their budget and they will do what they like with it. In fact the following quote illustrates that this is not really true:

> *Any amount made available by an LEA to the governing body;*
> *a) Shall remain the property of the authority until spent by the governing body or headteacher.*
> *b) When spent by the governing body or the headteacher, shall be taken to be spent by them as the authority's agent.*
> (School Standards and Framework Act, 1998 Section 49 (5))

Because of this legislation, local authorities can remove the delegated budget from a school if they believe that the school is not managing it properly. This sanction is only rarely applied, for example, if there is evidence of financial mismanagement or persistent failure to comply with the Scheme for Financing Schools.

Of course, schools can carry forward surpluses, and have to carry deficits forward to future years. Local authorities examine robustly how the school proposes to use this surplus, and if it exceeds 8 per cent of the budget share for primary (and special) schools, schools are normally asked to provide evidence that it is committed for some specific purpose. In extreme circumstances, the local authority may consider removing some of it and re-distributing it to other schools. The arrangements for deficits are covered in Chapter 3.

Reporting to parents

Although parents may ask specific questions about the budget, they are entitled to summary income and expenditure figures once a year, and will also be given further information as part of the Ofsted inspection report. Such figures normally appear as part of annual report to parents. A simple version is shown in Figure 7.1.

For the year ending 31 March 2006

Revenue income and expenditure

Income		Year ending 31–3–06 £	Year ending 31–3–05 £
1	Funds delegated by the LEA	614,126	557,195
2	Standards fund	104,907	118,998
3	Other grants	23,877	18,597
4	Income from receipts	56,638	65,960
5	Donations and private funds	12,278	5,490
6	**Total income**	811,826	766,240

Expenditure

7	Teaching staff salaries	406,583	390,172
8	Supply teaching staff salaries	9,051	2,767
9	Education support staff salaries	107,213	97,310
10	Other support staff salaries	64,868	54,831
11	Indirect staffing costs	13,673	14,486
12	Premises and site costs	48,333	43,847
13	Education learning resources costs	43,382	28,298
14	Other supplies and services	135,893	108,754
15	Direct revenue funding of capital expenditure	–	–
16	**Total expenditure**	828,996	740,465
17	**Revenue surplus/deficit (–)**	–17,170	25,775

Summary of capital transactions

Income		Year ending 31–3–06 £	Year ending 31–3–05 £
18	Capital income	26,750	21,867
19	Loans	–	–
20	Voluntary and private income	–	–
21	Direct revenue funding of capital expenditure	–	–
22	**Total funding**	26,750	21,867

Capital expenditure

23	Acquisition of land and buildings	–	–
24	New construction, conversion and renovation	15,000	15,000
25	Vehicles, plant, equipment and machinery	14,869	10,000
26	Other supplies and services	–	–
27	**Total expenditure**	29,869	25,000
28	**Capital surplus/deficit (–)**	–3,119	–3,133

Summary of unspent balances

		Revenue (£)	Capital (£)
29	Unspent balances brought forward as at 1–4–05	37,847	13,836
30	Surplus/deficit (–) for year ending 31–3–06	–17,170	–3,119
31	Unspent balance carried forward as at 31–3–06	20,677	10,717

Figure 7.1 Governors annual income and expenditure statement

Reporting to governors

Governors have a clear accountability for activities in a school, including the budget, which means that they should be able to explain what is going on, not necessarily in detail but enough to report the basics. They cannot do this if they are kept ignorant of the current budgetary situation.

Not all governors will require the financial information; it will depend on:

■ their role;

■ their level of interest and skills; and

■ whether the school budget presents problems.

Some may be content with the most basic of income and expenditure information, just enough to tell whether they are in surplus or deficit. Table 7.1 is an example of this.

However, some governors, particularly members of the finance committee or the chair of the governing body, are likely to need considerably more detail, including income and expenditure against different CFR headings, and differences between actual and expected income or expenditure. Many governors find the format of monitoring reports difficult; feedback from governors suggests that schools do not always take time to explain them clearly.

Table 7.1 An example of basic financial information

Financial information	Revenue funds (£)	Capital funds (£)
Total income	488,071	31,042
Total expenditure	416,724	21,868
Balance (surplus or deficit)	71,347	9,174
Last year's carryforward (surplus or deficit)	−9,000	4,500
Carryforward to next year (surplus or deficit)	62,347	13,674

You would be well advised to actually talk to your governors about what information they require and in what format it should be presented.

Contact your financial support services provider – they can often offer reporting formats adapted for the specific needs of your governors.

Reporting to the local authority

It is the responsibility of the school's governing body to manage planned levels of expenditure within their available resources and the local authority has to ensure that schools are doing just that. The local authority also has a statutory duty to ensure that public funds are spent effectively and to monitor financial management arrangements in schools.

It is for this reason that local authorities can require regular monitoring reports from schools. The Chief Financial Officer (CFO) has a statutory responsibility for the financial affairs of the local authority, including schools. In addition, recent guidance issued by the DfES in connection with the FMSiS, placed a requirement for the CFO to sign a declaration to the effect that relevant schools meet the FMSiS, following an external assessment.

The actual reporting requirements will vary from local authority to local authority, whether schools have their own separate financial accounts or use a central accounting system, and will be defined in the Scheme for Financing Schools mentioned in Chapter 3. Typically schools are required to submit the following returns.

Annual returns

■ A governor approved annual budget plan by a prescribed date in the late spring. Sometimes this requirement extends to a multi-year plan. This should be approved by the governing body and signed by the chair.

■ A confirmation that the Audit of Voluntary and Private Funds has been undertaken and signed by the independent auditors. The timing of this will depend on whether schools are accounting for the financial or calendar year.

■ A Best Value Statement, signed by the governors in line with section 3.7 of the FMSiS. This is an expression of the commitment of the school to achieving best value, and a summary of areas of the budget that the school intends to examine in the current financial year to ensure that this commitment is meaningful.

■ A Controls Assurance Statement in line with section 1.4 of the Financial Management Standard, considered by the governing body, and signed by the head and chair. R37 in the FMSiS Toolkit is a template for such a statement. This is an annual confirmation by the governors that they are assured that the processes are in place to ensure very effective financial management of the school and its resources.

Quarterly returns

■ A quarterly income and expenditure statement, usually at the end of June, September, December and March. Schools with significant financial difficulties may be asked to submit more frequent returns.

Monthly returns

■ A VAT return in the prescribed format. This is required in order for schools to reclaim VAT paid on purchases.

Reporting to the DfES

Schools must submit their Consistent Financial Reporting Return, which summarises income, expenditure, balances and surpluses for the outgoing financial year to the DfES. This is usually submitted in late April or early May and will either be forwarded to the DfES by the local authority, or can be submitted directly by the school via the DfES website.

■ Reporting on premises and health and safety

In fact, parents and trade unions are probably more likely to ask questions about the school building or health and safety, and of course both groups have a legitimate interest in these issues. Parents have recently asked probing questions of schools on a range of issues such as security fencing, the adequacy of sanitary arrangements, litter on the playing field and leaking roofs. Parents whose children are about to go on outdoor pursuits holidays are entitled to clear explanations of what safety precautions are in place, in advance of the trip. Such issues are common subjects for complaints; this can involve the school in considerable effort.

Preparing for an audit

Why and how often they can ask you for information

Internal audits can ask you for information about your accounting systems and processes as agents of the CFO of the local authority. Many local authorities will arrange internal audit visits every three to five years, but as it can be a lot longer between audit visits, some schools may have their systems audited remotely by examining the transactions (e.g. receipts and payments) in the central accounting system rather than a visit to the school.

What they will look for

Auditors usually work to a pre-agreed list of items to examine. Document S.5.2 'Internal Financial Controls' in the FMSiS Toolkit provides a useful checklist of the sort of areas that internal audit will explore. Auditors will usually look for 'audit trails' or evidence of steps in the process. For example, they are likely to examine the following typical areas.

Purchasing
They will seek evidence that schools have shopped around for value for money including quotes, produced specifications and orders, checked delivery, paid invoices, and recorded all this properly in the accounts.

Petty cash
They will check how the school deals with cash, whether receipts are given, if it is kept secure and banked promptly, signed for, and is recorded properly in the accounts.

Risk management

They will check that the school is auditing and recording the risks they face, including health and safety, and doing all they can to mitigate the possible effects of such risks by taking appropriate actions. Among the areas they might comment on are:

■ fire detection and prevention;

■ administration of medicines;

■ control of unauthorised exit from schools;

■ annual health and safety checks.

Although such areas might not seem to have financial consequences, the compensation culture we live in means that they often do.

Chapter 4 of this book outlines more about the internal control checks the auditors will undertake.

What happens next

Having conducted their audit, the internal auditors will typically present their findings in a written report. Usually you will have an opportunity to comment on it, and mistakes may be corrected. You should then share this report with the governors, ideally with the finance committee, and attach an action plan for resolving the issues they raise. It is important to stress that this is intended to be a constructive process, not a negative one. A copy of the report will usually be provided to the CFO or his or her representative in the local authority, who will use it, together with other similar reports, to form a view as to what gaps in general knowledge and skills there might be in schools.

■ Getting help

Choosing and training an administrator

Once upon a time primary administrators were secretaries who did a few administrative jobs on the side. Clerks typed a few letters and added up the dinner money. Today a school administrator needs to be a multi-skilled individual operating various ICT systems, often managing a group of staff, and sometimes having responsibility for buildings. Salaries and job titles have improved accordingly and there are relevant qualifications available through the National Bursars Association and improved training from both local authorities and commercial organisations. Support groups in many areas and even annual conferences covering the key issues of the day have somewhat mitigated the isolation that many school administrators have felt in the past.

However, some administrators have struggled to cope with the pace of change, particularly with so many new processes and ICT systems, and multi-tasking in a primary office is a continuing challenge. It isn't easy to complete the quarterly returns to the local authority while answering the main door, telephone and fax machine, fending off an angry parent and coping with little Kylie's nausea!

Part S1.3 of the FMSiS provide background information on the role of the bursar with access to relevant competencies (sections S2.1 and R11 of the FMSiS Toolkit). Although this will vary from school to school, this is a useful tool for appraisal and assessment of training needs, production of a job description and person specification, and consequent recruitment and selection. We should stress the importance of including administrative staff in an annual performance management or appraisal scheme, to identify their targets and ensure that they have the appropriate access to training and development.

In outline, the main competencies of a bursar are:

- ability to multi-task;
- extraction, analysis, interpretation and presentation of information;
- networking skills with other school administrative staff;
- knowledge of the financial situation of the school;
- understanding of internal control processes;
- numeracy skills;
- establishing relationships with other school staff;

- ability to pursue income generation;

- ability to deal with stakeholder questions etc.

In addition to ensuring that your administrator has appropriate skills, you also need to ensure that your administrator has adequate ICT equipment. It is understandably tempting to renew your ICT learning resources first, but financial tools are demanding in terms of processor speed and memory, and you should consider regular replacement.

Choosing and training a building superintendent/caretaker

The role of a caretaker, or more often now a building superintendent, has also changed. As well as locking up the building and supervising the cleaning, they are likely to be undertaking DIY jobs, and sometimes have professional skills like plumbing or electrics. As with administrators, training is vital and as such needs to be identified through a proper appraisal process.

Some schools will also use their building manager to select, monitor and review contractors, which raises further recruitment and skills issues. You may wish to look for candidates who have specialist, as well as general skills.

Useful website addresses

The environment in which schools manage their finance, buildings and health and safety is changing so quickly that up to date information is best found on the Internet and the following is a list of websites that you may find useful to update yourselves on school finance. The very best, such as the NCSL website, have interactive features to facilitate your learning. Many link to each other.

Audit Commission
www.audit-commission.gov.uk

DfES Value for Money Unit
www.dfes.gov.uk/valueformoney/

A direct source of information about financial issues, and has good links to the DfES Financial Management Standard, the Consistent Financial Reporting Framework, the national benchmarking website, Best Value, and training events.

Governornet – information for school governors
www.governornet.co.uk/

This website has a straightforward overview on school finance and property, covering roles and responsibilities, the law, with quick links to other topics.

National Bursars Association
www.nba.org.uk/

Key website for training of school administrative staff with advice on qualifications, details of development workshops, and a document library.

National College for School Leadership – financial management pages
www.ncsl.org.uk/

The NCSL website has a comprehensive set of e-learning materials on financial management and premises to download, including on-line scenarios to work through, frequently asked questions, and a resource library. It also has helpful links to other sites.

Teachernet
www.teachernet.gov.uk/
A vast website with a useful management section, with one of the most comprehensive guides to the complex subject of how schools are funded. It also has excellent health and safety materials. You can also gain access by a quick portal (or virtual access doorway) to the national finance benchmarking site, Supporting Schools' Financial Management (SSFM) website and to the FMSiS.

Index

For Product Safety Concerns and Information please contact our EU
representative GPSR@taylorandfrancis.com
Taylor & Francis Verlag GmbH, Kaufingerstraße 24, 80331 München, Germany